D0881135

Crosscurrents / MODERN CRITIQUES

Harry T. Moore, *General Editor*

Continuance and Change

The Contemporary
British Novel Sequence

Robert K. Morris

\ı ı

WITH A PREFACE BY

Harry T. Moore

SOUTHERN ILLINOIS UNIVERSITY PRESS
Carbondale and Edwardsville

FEFFER & SIMONS, INC.
London and Amsterdam

For Tony and Teddy,
who one day may understand history

Copyright © 1972 by Southern Illinois University Press
All rights reserved
Printed in the United States of America
Designed by Andor Braun
International Standard Book Number 0-8093-0544-5
Library of Congress Catalog Card Number 74-175951

Contents

Preface

In the present book Professor Robert K. Morris of City College examines the novel sequences of six British authors: Anthony Burgess, Lawrence Durrell, Doris Lessing, Olivia Manning, Anthony Powell, and C. P. Snow. The Crosscurrents/Modern Critiques series already lists studies of two of these authors, and books on two more of them are on the way; but in an overview such as Professor Morris's we are given certain perspectives not otherwise obtainable.

One of Professor Morris's principal themes is the concept of time as represented in these examples of what the French call the roman fleuve. Taking this as a key to the various sequences, he provides us with some unusually lucid insights, and the thoroughness with which he deals with the novels themselves makes his examination of them extremely valuable (though I think he somewhat underrates C. P. Snow, whom, however, he defends from various criticisms which have been made of him, particularly in regard to style). But because this is a work of criticism, the author doesn't give much space to the investigation of the backgrounds of these novels.

They must all be written under great strain, of the kind unknown to the majority of fiction writers, most of whose books are, in intention at least, not necessarily related: Dickens is a prime example of this. Of course the author of a long novel must know something of the strain the writer of serial volumes feels. Consider Tolstoy, for instance, whose fabulously long War and Peace is often thought of as the greatest of novels. The idea for it first came to him in 1863; he didn't finish the book until 1869. And there are many other examples.

At a quite different level, the writers of the television series known as soap operas have somewhat similar problems. Granted, these sentimentalized stories can have no depth, and their characters can't grow and change like those in serious literature. (It was interesting to see the serious television production of Hamlet with Richard Chamberlain, who for so many years had to be unfailingly sweet in the Dr. Kildare serial; he was a good Hamlet, and though he didn't express the implicit tragedy of the rôle he showed how different from Kildare he could be as he dealt in comic sarcasm with Claudius, Polonius, and Rosencrantz and Guildenstern.) Yet the soap-opera writers must keep their characters going from one interesting situation to another, just as serious authors must do.

Professor Morris begins with Doris Lessing, whose Martha Quest series, Children of Violence, is based upon Mrs. Lessing's own experiences as a young white girl from Southern Rhodesia (much of this material is used again in Mrs. Lessing's intricately organized novel, The Golden Notebook, which Irving Howe has called— rightly, I think—one of the finest works of fiction since the Second World War). Professor Morris then takes up Olivia Manning's Balkan Trilogy, in which an English couple, Guy and Harriet Pringle, undergo complex and tense experiences in wartime Bucharest and Athens. It is only natural that Professor Morris takes us next to an even more exotic setting with Lawrence Durrell's Alexandria Quartet. Durrell, incidentally, is the subject of a critical collection in the Crosscurrents series, The World of Lawrence Durrell.

Anthony Burgess is considered next in this book, with his Malayan Trilogy, in its American edition called The Long Day Wanes; as Professor Morris points out, it is one of the important pictures of the collapse of the British Empire. Note that all the authors he has so far discussed project exotic settings. The next two writers, C. P. Snow and Anthony Powell, focus mainly on England, Snow in Strangers and Brothers and Powell in A Dance to the Music of Time. The author of the present volume believes that the latter series is the finest of them all, although it is not yet completed: the story of Nicholas Jenkins and the infernally reappearing Widmerpool. Jenkins is the narrator, as Lewis Eliot is in Snow's sequence, which seems to me to have a wider scope than any of these other sets of novels, covering as it does the worlds of law, science, and government, among others. Snow's series took the longest time in composition; the idea of it occurred to him at the beginning of 1935, and the first volume appeared in 1940; the Second World War caused a seven-year delay until the second book appeared, and the last item in the series came out in 1970.

In the course of this Preface I have commented critically only on C. P. Snow, in its second paragraph, also the subject of a Crosscurrents volume; as far as the other writers go, the reader is free to take up the chapters that follow with no more introduction than the faint outlines given in that paragraph and in the four following it. I think that Professor Morris's work should be approached freshly and immediately, for it is a fine critical study which presents its own approaches and follows them up skillfully.

HARRY T. MOORE

Southern Illinois University
November 25, 1971

Acknowledgments

I wish to thank the following publishers for allowing me to use quotations from their books:

From *The Great Fortune* by Olivia Manning, copyright © 1960 by Olivia Manning. Reprinted by permission of Doubleday & Company, Inc.; and also by permission of William Heinemann, Ltd., the British publisher.

From *The Spoilt City* by Olivia Manning, copyright © 1962 by Olivia Manning. Reprinted by permission of Doubleday & Company, Inc.; and also by permission of William Heinemann, Ltd., the British publisher.

From *Friends and Heroes* by Olivia Manning, copyright © 1965 by Olivia Manning. Reprinted by permission of Doubleday & Company, Inc.; and also by permission of William Heinemann, Ltd., the British publisher.

From *The Alexandria Quartet* by Lawrence Durrell. Copyright © 1957, 1958, 1960 by Lawrence Durrell. Reprinted by permission of E. P. Dutton & Co.; and also by permission of Faber and Faber, Ltd., the British publishers.

From *Martha Quest* by Doris Lessing, copyright © 1952, 1954, 1964 by Doris Lessing. Reprinted by permission of Simon and Schuster; and also by permission of Curtis Brown, Ltd., the British publisher.

From *Landlocked* by Doris Lessing, copyright © 1958, 1965, 1966 by Doris Lessing. Reprinted by permission of Simon and Schuster; and also by permission of Curtis Brown, Ltd., the British publisher.

From *The Golden Notebook* by Doris Lessing, copyright ©

1962 by Doris Lessing. Reprinted by permission of Simon and Schuster; and also by permission of Michael Joseph, Ltd.

From *The Four-Gated City* by Doris Lessing, copyright © 1969 by Doris Lessing Productions Ltd. Reprinted by permission of Alfred A. Knopf, Inc.; and also by permission of Curtis Brown, Ltd., the British publisher.

From *The Collected Works of Paul Valéry*, ed. Jackson Matthews, Bollingen Series XLV, vol. 8, *Leonardo, Poe, Mellarmé*, trans. by Malcolm Cowley and James R. Lawler. Copyright © 1972 by Princeton University Press. Also by permission of Routledge & Kegan Paul.

From *A Question of Upbringing, A Buyer's Market, The Acceptance World, Casanova's Chinese Restaurant, The Kindly Ones, The Soldier's Art,* and *The Military Philosophers*, all by Anthony Powell, reprinted by permission of Little, Brown and Company; and also by permission of William Heinemann, Ltd., the British publisher.

From *On Violence* by Hannah Arendt, reprinted by permission of Harcourt, Brace & World, Inc.; and also by permission of Penguin Books, Ltd.

From *The Long Day Wanes* by Anthony Burgess, reprinted by permission of W. W. Norton and Company.

From *Time for a Tiger, Enemy in the Blanket,* and *Beds in the East* by Anthony Burgess, reprinted by permission of William Heinemann, Ltd.

From *Strangers and Brothers* by C. P. Snow, reprinted by permission of Charles Scribner's Sons; and also by permission of St. Martin's Press, New York; the Macmillan Company of Canada; and Macmillan & Co., Ltd.

Portions of Chapter 6 appeared in *The Novels of Anthony Powell*, copyright © 1968, University of Pittsburgh Press.

Portions of Chapter 4 appeared in *The Consolations of Ambiguity: An Essay on the Novels of Anthony Burgess*, Copyright © 1971 by the Curators of the University of Missouri.

Introduction

"The folly of mistaking a paradox for a discovery," writes Paul Valéry in his *Introduction to the Method of Leonardo da Vinci*, "and a metaphor for proof . . . is inborn in us." The present study, proceeding from a paradoxical title which sets itself up as critical metaphor, is not offered to flaunt this lucid, paralyzing truth, nor—hopefully —to obscure either proof or discovery. Its much more modest aim is to show how two major concepts of time— continuance and change—are at the heart of a half dozen varied, unique, and important novel sequences, all written within the last fifteen years by leading British novelists.

Using so elusive and volatile an abstraction as time for measuring certain solid critical observations can scarcely be called original and may indeed be considered suspect. There is, however, perhaps no form more susceptible to a time-ordered view than the series novel or (as it is often called in deference to its French origins) *roman fleuve.* Not merely concerned with time's compression and expansion, its subjective and objective, psychical and physical workings—for in the last analysis what novel isn't?— the novel sequence links moment-by-moment personal change with expanding historic change and projects both against a backdrop flowing on relentlessly and continually.

In the most flexible of ways the novel sequence is fiction's flirtation with etiology, riveting one eye on patterns of time, the other on patterns of timelessness, while focusing both on the causes and reasons for the individual's moral, aesthetic, psychological or social growth. While no writer at hand can be called either historian or metaphysician, none of the sequences can escape implications of history or metaphysics. History is, after all, the most logical biography of man in all his roles; and history —despite attempts to prove the contrary—must necessarily always be the ordained slave of time.

One setting out to provide an overall critique of this rather special—and in recent years phenomenal—novelistic form might have proposed some revealing distinction between the art of history that fictionalizes and the art of fiction that historicizes. But fascinating as the approach might have been, it would seem—in the last analysis—irrelevant and ambiguous. Certainly no novelist concerned with past, present, and future can escape grappling with history. Even the most recluse, aesthetic, antihistoric (and probably greatest) writer of the *roman fleuve*, Marcel Proust, whose *Remembrance of Things Past* is a paen to the art that consumed him and to the society that fed his art, incorporated about fifty years of French history into his monumental series. Yet Proust— like the six writers under discussion—is first and foremost an artist, shaping history according to his own quirky view of time and through his own ecstatic vision of art.

History, then, acts as a double agent, the shaper of events as well as the events shaped. In addition to widening the dimensions of the novel sequence by increasing the range of movement and interaction of characters, it fashions a framework for causes and contingencies of historical fact (generally opaque and complex) that will be transformed into illuminating fictional truths. But why the novel sequence is neither historicized fiction nor fictionalized history is identical in both cases. A work of art, by transcending facts as such, transcends history.

To say that none of these writers is transcribing history *per se* is not to ignore how certain underlying assumptions—as distinguished from mere reflections—about history pervade each series as a whole. Yet with the possible exception of Doris Lessing (who was for many years a Communist) and C. P. Snow (whose scientific training has made him a student of procedures whereby things are "worked out"), none fosters a philosophy of history that does not bear directly upon the particular artistic method being used. Were one to compare the body of historical facts with its corresponding novelistic treatment, the obvious conclusion would be to state rather baldly that history evolves from art, rather than vice versa. But this may well anticipate the assumptions themselves.

The first assumption is that as they play upon sensibilities, the historical background is generally dominated by the fictional foreground. Interwoven or running parallel, historic time functions less forcefully than fictional time because the historic moment seems only an enlargement of the protagonists' world view. That the *Malayan Trilogy* of Anthony Burgess portrays the futility of history owes less to any political or sociological theories on the rise and fall of emergent nations—though obviously Burgess's knowledge on all counts is full—than to the personality of his hero gripped by circumstances he has in part created but for which, in the end, he must take full responsibility. The quest after permanence by Olivia Manning's young heroine is accentuated by wartime conditions in Budapest and Athens but is in the end, one imagines, a response conditioned by her cultural recalcitrance, certain kind of upbringing, and romantic naïveté; it is as though the historic problem were created by Mrs. Manning to enact the personal challenge. And one of the most memorable descriptions in all of Anthony Powell—the delicate movements of Field Marshal Montgomery's hands over a war map that "was no less than a great slice of history"—is a crystallization of the hand warfare of saluting, waving, shuffling, prodding, dialing, and nudging the hand of fate found throughout the war trilogy of *The Music of Time* and throughout all wars.

The second assumption reflects the writers' resistance to directly dramatizing the large-scale historic event. The indirect use of material—what one might call an oblique historic positioning within the narrative posture—results in a heightening of particulars and a fogging of generalities. World War II, for example, an experience generally shared among the sequences, is never played onstage. As Hannah Arendt has pointed out, the great tremors of history are but interruptions of the steady, normal movements of humanity. Consequently, the novel that would emphasize character and theme over idea or action must never allow an incident of history to exceed in scope or brilliance a character's perception of it. Personalization of an event, at greatest remove from the so-called realism of Hugo, Tolstoy or Zola, whose plunge into revolutions and war dwarfed their personae and often made them mere symbolic ciphers in the greater tally, is one of the few remaining methods left the novelist to sustain without interruption the continuum of time against which individual change is traced.

One final assumption bears on the relationship of setting to history and emphasizes the important difference between the logic of history and the logic of fiction. Like the historian, the novelist may begin with identical premises and through various refinements of construction, interpretation, sensitivity, and intelligence arrive at very different conclusions. Something of this may be seen in the sequences of Mrs. Manning and Burgess, both very broadly concerned with disillusionment and disintegration of an ideal, but one valiantly optimistic where the other is quietly and ironically futile.

Unlike the historian's, however, the fabric of the novelist's argument is not destroyed in the contravening of any single, linking premise. The conclusion, that is, becomes an entity almost independent of the premises, interesting and valid in itself. Snow's assertions about the English upper and middle classes, while vastly different from Powell's anatomy of the same classes, in no way actually conflicts with it. Yet while both men write about roughly the same structures and the same period in history—from World War I to the present—the England of one is not only dissimilar from the England of the other, but so dissimilar as to be almost unrecognizable. Accusing the novelist who transforms history of playing with it unfairly becomes, however, a critical pursuit more chimerical than the novelist's chase through time itself. Forever vulnerable to frontal attack on his perverting the logic of history, the writer of the *roman fleuve* must advance or retreat by the theory that logic, just like aesthetics, evolves from an ethos generated within the novel and from nowhere else.

Since the art of the novel sequence has not received the same attention as the "art of the novel," it is difficult to know how successfully this particular ethos has been realized. For some critics the sequence novel is not really *a* novel at all, but a number of books loosely strung together. For others it is *a* novel, but at its most infirm, hobbling along, with history as a kind of telescoping crutch that can be lengthened or shortened at whim should the author's fancy or imagination give out. The intention of this study is neither to anticipate nor counter such objections but to suggest that through a consistent (perhaps overly single-minded) preoccupation with a challenging motif—continuance and change—a sequence, in the same way as a novel, may be approached critically as an entity among equals while remaining *sui generis*.

The springboard for this view is constructed to be both

sturdy and flexible, though it is not the only purchase for the leap into time and history. An equally long book could be organized about other principal motifs: the image and impact of society upon the individual; the quest after a vanishing ideal; the search for a personal *modus vivendi* within the social and political *modus operandi*; the closing circle of freedom in an age constricted with varieties of determinism—an admittedly existential proposition; or, finally, the displacement of the glorious myths of humanity by the ogre called history.

Disregarding for a moment the question of ethos, one could view these sequences as specimens of *Bildungsroman*, with the long and incessant growth of the protagonist perhaps of a higher order than his conflict with change. Style, of course, is another matter. Anyone who has read several or all of the works will feel that one novelist writes better than another, or at least with more energy and force. Mrs. Lessing's prose is far and away more intense and charged than Snow's, Powell is wittier than either, and Burgess, despite his punning excesses and Joycean influences, is more verbally agile than all three together. That style, like content, is intimately involved with form is too old a critical hat for reblocking here. But how one actually affects the other is a new and complex matter when related to the novel sequence. Here, certainly, is a subject that must be worked out at a later date.

Paying lip service in a brief introduction to what could have been done may strike some as the worst sort of apology for not having done it. The subjunctive is not merely an unwieldy tense but a dangerous state of mind. And even to say that the subsequent criticism has tangentially worked in the above cluster of suggestions may seem no less suspect. If any justification is needed for what has or has not been included, it must be that the overriding idea of continuance and change is broad enough to embrace most aspects of the sequences without forcing comparisons of a qualitative nature. What each writer attempts in his sequence is different. Admittedly, the *raison d'être* is not always the best reason, but it is all one has. The critic must comply with what the novelist considers the particular function of his series and not with what he feels the function ought to have been. While comparisons must necessarily emerge, while criticism might seem at times even sharp, each sequence in the end rises or falls by its own merits.

For this reason the critical methods vary with the sequences themselves. One dare not approach Snow with the same critical tools used for Durrell; in the first case one is working with textures, in the second with an amazing interplay of motif and imagery. Again, writers are generally dissimilar over similarities. Powell's treatment of the artist in *The Music of Time* is not only vastly different from Durrell's, but in no way bears as directly on the sequence as a whole. Nor is Durrell's concern with revolution as central to the *Quartet* as Mrs. Lessing's is to *Children of Violence*. Subtract "revolution" from the former and an interesting, but not vital variation is lost; subtract it from the latter and the entire framework breaks down. By the same token one may almost completely ignore Burgess's comic relief without violating the impetus or thrust of the *Malayan Trilogy*, yet without a rather careful understanding of Mrs. Manning's use of the comic protagonist in her trilogy the point of it may be almost entirely obscured.

As the critical methods vary, so the critical emphasis varies as well. Discussions of Burgess and Mrs. Manning center about plot as much as theme, primarily because their sequences are least known in the United States, but also because much of the action in itself supports shifting conceptions of time and change. The notions entertained about the *Alexandria Quartet* may seem at variance with problems of time and history unless it becomes clear almost at once that Durrell's treatment of art is as much a problem of the historic, as the aesthetic, sensibility. The strong—some may consider it over-strong —preoccupation with Martha Quest in *Children of Violence* is imperative for placing her in direct conflict with the forces that would repress her, the tensions that would weaken her, the ideologies that would demoralize her, the habits that would dull her, the men who would absorb her. And with Powell and Snow one must emphasize form simply because while one writer has been nearly totally successful in reconciling the physical movements of life with the metaphysical propositions of time, the other has seemed at odds with both conditions.

In any case the essays have tried to incorporate as much criticism about the individual novels themselves as about their place in the sequence, or, for that matter, about the sequence in its supportive illustration of continuance and change. These ideas, after all, are no mere isolated phenomena drummed up in order to make several points about the contemporary British novel. They are—reiterating an observation made at the opening of this introduction—the paradoxes from which one seeks discovery and the metaphor from which one seeks proof. The most important realization lies beyond any critical assumptions or methods, beyond readings or explications. Even at their most pessimistic, these six writers seem in agreement, if only on one point. Man, the sport of flux and uncertainty, remains the fallible but sole hope for discovering within himself and within the inexorable patterns of continuance, proof that something may at last order what appears more and more for our age those frightening, radical, and destructive forces of change.

ROBERT K. MORRIS

Denmark, Maine

Summer, 1971

Continuance and Change

1

Doris Lessing
Children of Violence: The Quest for Change

"Living in the midst of this whirlwind of change it is impossible to make final judgments or absolute statements of value." Thus writes Doris Lessing, an exiled Southern Rhodesian and ex-Communist who, for nearly twenty years, has been concerned with man as a societal double agent, at once "isolated . . . unable to communicate, helpless and solitary," yet at the same time "collective . . . with a collective conscience." [1]

Mrs. Lessing's dualistic outlook is born of experiences that connect with the significant tremors of our century —at least those of the last generation and a half. Growing up in Southern Rhodesia's aridity of culture and innundations of morality, amidst its cloying conformity and hypocrisy, under the pressures of its class snobbism among colonials and its racial antagonism between blacks and whites, she has weathered the major crises of between the wars, failing to be satisfied either by the Marxian way in or the existentialist way out. Her reticence to be final or absolute, her just suspicion of historic pigeonholing are therefore not too surprising. She has tried to see personal and social conflicts removed from dry dogmatism, glib pragmatism, or unimpeachable but generally unworkable philosophies, and to gain an objective but passionate view of man by examining the "individual conscience in its relation with the collective" at those points of rest operating within the eye of the storm.

This has, again and again, been the theme of most of her prolific writing, best developed in two works: the energetic, skillful, somewhat overweight but immensely forceful *Golden Notebook*, and her extraordinary novel sequence, *Children of Violence*. The first weaves a complex fabric of the sexual, political, and artistic growth of Anna Wulf, a woman writer who keeps five notebooks simultaneously and is writing a novel about a woman who is writing a novel. *The Golden Notebook* is technically less adroit than *The Counterfeiters* (which Gide pulled off with the minimum of *longeurs*), or *The Death of Virgil* (which Broch inflated with the maximum of poetic instinct), and in the long run less satisfying or comprehensive—and perhaps somewhat less relevant—than *Children of Violence* which works equally well as *Bildungsroman*, autobiography, political and social history, science fiction and prophecy, and as a tentative statement of a writer committed to (and consequently alienated from) our age.

Children of Violence traces through five volumes the progress of Martha Quest from her girlhood in Southern Rhodesia ("Zambesia" in the sequence) through her two marriages, her motherhood, her membership in the Communist party, her life in England, and ultimately her death there as one of the world's multimillions wiped out in the 1990s by a series of nuclear and nerve-gas holocausts. Martha is, in all respects, the right sort of "individual conscience"—liberal, pacifistic, self-conscious, troubled, aware, sensitive, naïve—an intellectual, emotional, political, and social being in confrontation with the collective, namely, all those things she has emerged from and all those things she wishes to grow into. She is a child of the times, experiencing perpetual change in an era of unchanging global violence brought about through revolution, racism, limited war, and finally the "Catastrophe," though these are less central to the sequence than the inward and outward changes Martha undergoes in her relationships with family, friends, mentors, husbands, and lovers. What she quests after is certitude, completeness, noncomplexity, and the freedom to "stand by what one is, how one sees things" without destroying others. Her desire at any time along the route is to submit her will to a collective if not the collective, but never finally, and to insist on making her own "personal and private judgments before every act of submission." Each crisis of identity creates her anew; yet each new creation becomes an act of survival protracting her hopeless quest. For over the far-ranging, impossible dream of racial brotherhood and sanity, a golden age lived in the "shining . . . golden . . . ideal city," the distressed and tormented nightmare of twentieth-century violence gallops roughshod toward apocalypse.

Though her great theme is violence, Mrs. Lessing writes coolly, dispassionately, logically, using the standard novelistic techniques of repetition, reinforcement, and — until the final plunge into the future in volume five — strict chronology. Seldom is she self-indulgent, save for an occasional sortie into Lawrencean impressionism when filling in the beauty or bleakness of a landscape, or in describing varieties of sexual tension. Her prose, however, is never as obliquely charged or — surprising for a poet — as poetic as Lawrence's, but direct and explicit, even when rhapsodic. Such predictability and dispassion lend a certain aura of disenchantment to long sections of the series, and the virtue of fidelity often points up an irritating flaw: a scrupulous exactitude for telling Martha's every germinating hope or fear in the early volumes and for setting down her emotional and political dialogues in the later ones. And all this free of innuendo, surprise, or comedy. Like Snow's, Mrs. Lessing's work attains a kind of suprarealism, but unlike his, her style is not a matter of inability to flog language into novelistic servitude. Rather we have a bold attempt at showing how an intelligence theoretically primed for every commitment fails before the actuality of the commitment itself. Martha—particularly in her obsession to be free— is cast ironically, though it is evident that the author sides with her heroine more often than against her, the gap between them bridged as much by sympathy as by the preoccupation of rationalizing Martha's every act.

Many of these excesses are purged in the first volume, *Martha Quest*, which sketches the outlines of a frustrated, informed girl who will later mythically swell into a woman of strength and despair. The novel, too, establishes the themes necessary for Martha's violent reactions to all who would formulate her, who would *force* her participation in one collective or another.

We first meet her at fifteen, sitting on the steps of her father's run-down farm reading Havelock Ellis (!) while her mother and a neighbor gossip about "servants, children, cooking, scandal." She is, we discover, restive, confined, resentful, passionate (incipiently), intellectually curious, but also a bit of an intellectual snob; she feels fated and doomed, opposed to her parents because in them she senses the habitual, the usual, and, should she fail to break away, the continuing.

> She was adolescent, and therefore bound to be unhappy; British, and therefore uneasy and defensive; in the fourth decade of the twentieth century, and therefore inescapably beset with problems of race and class; female, and obliged to repudiate the shackled woman of the past. She was tormented with guilt and responsibility and self consciousness; and she did not regret the torment.[2]

From here on she is to bring to bear on the march of events these reactions and patterns of behavior that grow out of the struggle between passivity and rebellion, mind and body, as she rejects recurring sets of values in hopes of defining others.

The early struggles of Martha that carry greatest weight are internal. She is alone, wishing to reach out and radiate outward, but not yet connecting. "Everything decayed and declined and leaned inward," she analyzes, without misgiving but with a sense of her own strivings and an awareness of the counterforces holding her back. Her desire at this point is to change at whatever cost. Change is choice; choice comes by way of freedom; and both stem from intimations of her own "smallness and unimportance" in the chaos and confusion of Zambesia, born of such abstractions as *"black, white, nation, race."* Indeed, chaos and confusion will transform the existential, thinking Martha into the essential, acting one before it destroys the very world in which she has struggled to survive and to understand.

The transformation is handled skillfully, if not always economically. Mrs. Lessing has brought to bear on Martha's development a romantic overview of the convulsive ethos in which she lives—an awakening and quickening prior to transformation. Martha's sense of being comes first from "things": her lone walks (taboo, of course) through the kopjes, books, physical presences, delight in her body freed from the puerility and titillation that apparently comprise much of the sexual staple among colonials. What Martha intuits, then intellectualizes, then refeels is the helplessness and vulnerability of a single person in the world, a need and affinity for sympathy and help. Rebellion may not necessarily mean change, but the desire for change is rebellion, especially that desire generated by universal impulses of love. Here, in a way, is the Wordsworthian prelude orchestrated anew. Mrs. Lessing seems to suggest that from such pantheism grows Martha's later commitment to communism, and beyond that—even as Martha's vision of the world grows darker—a communal belief in the human race, that it must survive through and because of people like herself; for "if she was feeling something, in this particular way, with the authenticity, the irresistibility, of the growing point, then she was not alone, others were feeling the same, since the growing point was never, could never be, just Martha's, could not be only the property or territory of one individual. No, if she experienced and was asking questions, then others like her were experiencing and asking questions: others looked for her as she looked for them." [3]

Yet in *Children of Violence* "growth" and "change" are made more synonymous than they ought be, the distinction between them is more blurred than it should be, or they are both written off by the author. Martha is flung into everwidening circles of experience, from the most basic unit (the family) into those more complex collectives—it is, of course, the way anyone does grow—with her ego the sole measurement of change. One group (the term is Mrs. Lessing's), one structure, one ideology, then another, offers a way of life potentially attractive, sound, certain; but all are ultimately disillusioning, unable to satisfy those inherently mystical, partially absurd and chaotic longings and stirrings within Martha; that sense of being alive and knowing it, and wanting something, someone to prove it. Anthony Powell's Nicholas Jenkins has similar qualitative experiences, but his orientation is toward becoming the perfect social being despite the muddle. Martha is intent on maintaining her individuality at any expense, becoming an outlaw from upbringing, class, society, country, and at last the human race as we have uncomfortably come to know it. At the finish of the sequence—somewhere around 1990—Martha (an elderly survivor of the "Catastrophe") ends her quest as part of a primitive, almost aboriginal collective grubbing for existence on a remote island off the Scottish coast. She is a freakish vestige of all the idealists of our time who looked for sanity and happiness at "the growing point," a parody of change in a world that now evolves rapidly through mutation, a world of monsters created out of our own monstrosity.

While little in the early sections of the sequence actually foreshadows the substance of its grim coda—particularly grim since overkill and its consequences daily grow less improbable and more comprehensible—Mrs. Lessing's intent to demolish all the illusions that thinly (or falsely) sustain the structure of our lives is pretty clear. Throughout the first two volumes she sets up and knocks down the groups unable to fulfill Martha's ideal: the farm families, budding intellectuals, secretaries, the Sports Club, housewives, mothers, and so forth. The technique at times becomes something of a bowling match, with its share of strikes, spares, misses, and long breathers in between. For the isolated experience is not —cannot be in so categorically realistic a novel—all that vital. Too, Martha's reactions are distressingly uniform (withdrawal, introspection, petulance, anger, pessimism, optimism at starting anew), and her reasons for rejecting what she does are apparent from the beginning. It is less a matter of committed conscience than absolute normalcy for a sensitive, alert, thinking woman to reject utterly the randy or dull or dowdy lots of people, and the conditions and ideologies (as Mrs. Lessing presents them) of Zambesian middle-class life. In the long run, however, such overthorough spadework is necessary, not only to enforce Martha's disillusionment, but to further Mrs. Lessing's notion that the catastrophes of life are too often meaninglessly (but humanly) obscured by its banalities.

There is, for example, the normal relationship between Martha and her parents, people not really awful, but standard and ordinary. It is not so much they, however, as their way of life—the way of life of moral, insular, puritanical, resigned and defeated colonials—that she rejects, and their marriage based on "ironic mutual pity," though it is precisely this condition (the human condition?) that will cement her deeper relationships later on. Martha's feelings of *odi-amo* for the Quests, too, reflect more than mere rebellious adolescence. They become the archetype for her feelings for many people. As soon as she becomes established in any way she feels closed in, desperately seeks escape, even though suffering compassion for those she wishes to escape from. Universal feelings of love too often prove inadequate guarantees against personal dislikes, mistrusts, and fears.

Martha rejects the patterns of family life. She also shuns at this time the catechisms of Solly and Joss Cohen, "one a Zionist, the other a Socialist." Both the Cohens are abstract reasoners on historic problems, members of a minority that will suffer in the debacle of a more widespread and virulent racism, but they heel too closely to the ritual of their own ideologies. Ritual, Mrs. Lessing implies, is part habit, part myth. The Quests, because they are colonials, must be as they are—part of the South African pioneer heritage. The Cohens, as left-wing educated Jews, sons of a merchant father, must be intellectuals and liberals, just as Martha herself must be a rebel, or, by turns, nothing, because once rebellion is ritualized it, too, becomes effete.

Martha's affiliations and defections deploy after a fashion into truisms, though Martha persists in the belief that one can remain individual, can find oneself apart from ritual. Thus she courts change for its own sake, not yet realizing that constant change can be as stultifying and dangerous as no change at all. Curiously enough—curious because in style, design, and result two writers could scarcely be more dissimilar—Harriet Pringle of Olivia Manning's *Balkan Trilogy* comes closer than Martha to Mrs. Lessing's implicit position. Though both heroines think of themselves first as individuals, then as women; though both alternate between cautious optimism and transcendental self-determination — Harriet has pluck, Martha studies Whitman and Thoreau as one might study the Bible or Marshall McLuhan, for inspiration, not for facts; though both somehow initially believe that by solving the problems of life one might uncover its meaning, they are antithetical in their *raisons d'être*. The one, living under sieges of uncertainty in war-torn Rumania and Athens, puts faith in permanence as the sole saving and stabilizing force, the true basis for "answering life"; the other (in her own mind at least) always operating under the shadow of "that great bourgeois monster repetition," sees the answer in change, and change alone.

The mode of *Children of Violence* does, then, as Mrs. Lessing requires of it, grow out of Martha's individual conscience. Change is a continuing phenomenon and the *modus vivendi* for Martha, more active than the comparatively passive Harriet. As false start succeeds false start, disillusion mounts upon disillusion, groping yields to groping, and one quest supplants another, Martha, who, however fumblingly, rebels from stasis, plunges repeatedly into error and dejection, sometimes into illumination and happiness at striving to become the ideal woman leading the new, good life.

In this Mrs. Lessing serves her heroine richly, but not unambiguously. An intellectual believing in social and personal progress, equality, fulfillment, and enlightenment as antidotes to virulence, she is also a novelist with an uncomfortable tendency to portray rather ghastly people whom one cannot really care about at all. Much of the sympathy for the idea of change on the social level seems vitiated by the realization that there appears little chance for change on the personal level. Too many of

Mrs. Lessing's "good" characters are so flat, humorless, weak, aimless, obtuse, and nasty that only a DNA revolution would seem capable of restructuring them.

There are the women, distinguishable from each other, yet seldom distinctive; quickened by a bit of gossip, a child, an impulse, a good deed, or a male, only to flag, flicker, fade into a stereotyped shadow. There is Marnie Rensberg the bovine Afrikaans flapper; Jasmine Cohen, the pretty, fiery radical who settles for a complacent upper-class marriage (a way Martha will never be); Mrs. Talbot, wealthy, conservative who tries to lure, then rope Martha into the reactionary fold; Mrs. Van, wealthy, liberal, who veils behind her welfare activities the philosophy of *festina lente* in volatile Zambesia; and Maisie, the girl from the lower classes, of easy virtue and heart of gold, who becomes an ideological battleground for Martha and Mr. Maynard.

Such women are set, and consequently static. By dint of her ability to grow and change—or to recognize that she can—Martha patently outstrips them. But there is more to it than that. One feels that these women often function merely as foils for Martha rather than as characters in themselves, and that Mrs. Lessing's large and expansive talent is weakened in making way for final revelations—the limitations of the *Bildungsroman* in any case. She is uneasy when turning ordinary experiences into profound ones. Of the women in the first four volumes, only May Quest, Martha's mother (singled out for a brief, brilliant study in *Landlocked*), in reviewing her past as a disappointed and frustrated wife and mother, momentarily soars above the flatlands of Zambesian womanhood. The strength and fullness of Mrs. Lessing's characters, it would seem, depend on the darkness of their plight. Thus, she creates her most successful character in *The Four-Gated City* with Lynda Coldridge, another wife and mother, tortured and shattered but

lacking Mrs. Quest's ability to hold on, whose schizo-
phrenia acts as a symbolic barometer for the madness of
the world without.

Mrs. Lessing is more successful with her men, and
more devastating about them. Most are flagrantly as-
sertive or perennially juvenile, sustained by the wives or
mistresses they generally consider inferior, on the whole
either sexually incompetent or fiercely brutal and selfish
about the sexual act of possession. There is the swish,
epicene Donovan Anderson, Martha's first beau upon
coming down from the farm; Binkie Maynard, the ersatz, twenty-years-behind-the-times-sports-clubbing Fitz-
geraldian; the slick, whining Adolph King (Martha's first
lover); Jack, the painter whom she sees in London and
whose satyr-like sexual appetite drives him to degrada-
tion; the quasi-sensitive, refined, but ultimately insipid
and hysterical thirty-year-old virgin, Douglas Knowell
(her first husband); the dour, deliberate, somewhat fa-
natic Communist Anton Hesse (her second husband);
Thomas Stern, the virile, melancholy, nihilistic, aggres-
sively radical wanderer who becomes the great passion
of Martha's life; and Mark Coldridge, a writer of bound-
less energy, infected and inflamed by dreams of brotherhood and peace, who takes over Thomas's legacy and
creates the "shining city," first in fiction, then in reality.

The ironically recurrent patterns traced by Martha in
her relationships with both women and men more often
than not frustrate her quest, impede her flight from the
"monster repetition" dogging her heels. With no woman
can she identify, with none can she keep alive a permanent, working friendship; from none can she draw the
model for the ideal woman she wishes to become, at least
not in the sane way she had always imagined. Her most
enduring bond is with the mad Lynda, for in their ses-
sions of madness together they seek confirmation of
themselves and escape from the general madness of the

world. The identical "ironic mutual pity" draws her to certain types of men. Yet from none of her husbands or lovers can she obtain personal or sexual satisfaction; from none gain a sense of solidity; from none retrieve fragments of self abandoned and lost to another.

This pattern of relationships creates immense problems for Martha, who, more and more, appears reacting in a vacuum or negatively. Change she does, from the sensible, naïve, idealistic, interested, involved, educable girl to the wiser, more harried, more intractable, tenacious and vital woman, seeing what she does *not* want, not seeing what she wants. "I will not be like this," she says of practically everyone, the plea and credo growing hollower as she cuts off choices, as rebellion dissipates into compulsiveness, monotony, and habit, as she finds it increasingly more difficult to restore her personality through "acts of survival."

The overall irony of Martha's plight is that she is forced into a dialogue of one without proper antiphonal response. Even those who mold her most fully—Thomas, Lynda, Mark—are too involved in defining or destroying themselves to be of sustaining influence. Eventually Martha's fears, her disastrous liaisons, her failed ideals, seem as patent and predetermined and usual as the people and ideals from which she is in revolt. Why, one might ask, does so much of the action in the sequence either confirm the philosophy of the cynical Mr. Maynard—"the more things change, the more they remain the same"—or blunder toward the catastrophe in which the only change that can come about is attended by worldwide decimation? Is Martha a dupe of her era? of the author? of change itself, forever a fiction and never a reality? Is it that the *fact*, rather than the *idea* of change has become suspect to Mrs. Lessing? Or is it simply recognizing the dead-end in changing when no one else does, realizing that all change is futile if the human race is fated to eventually go up in the big bang?

These rhetorical splinters are, as Mrs. Lessing understands, imbedded not merely in the rough grain of *Children of Violence,* but in the anxieties our age has fashioned for us, and are thrust into solid projections of a
single, complex question: What may we, as individuals,
accept or reject insofar as our volition, needs, and conscience are concerned; what can we at any time reject or
accept as part of any collective? The answer is paramount
for dictating the means and ends of change, the efficacy
of it as much as the desire for it. Our century has shown
the individual conscience much more frequently operating against, rather than with the collective. "Us" has
become one monolithic entity, "them" another, a negativism not only intolerable, but unworkable, self-defeat-
ing, hateful. As Mrs. Lessing enforces throughout her sequence, knowledge gained in a vacuum is false knowledge; "know thyself" is no longer a viable philosophy,
limited as we are in our capabilities to alone effect
change. We must also—primarily—apprehend the truth
of and about others and about the realities of the world,
not as they would or should exist, but as they do. This
is the first and ultimate step in bringing about a change
that will preserve individual and collective alike, decently
and nobly.

Part of Martha's quest is just this, apprehending the
sense of others—through individuals and groups—and
struggling free of the negativism that has a stranglehold
on her development. In her search for an ideal identity
there are nominal realities Martha readily grasps. She
will not stagnate; she will fight repetition, loose the "deterministic chain," resist becoming part of a cycle that
grinds on from generation to generation; she will challenge all cynics who find in (personal) failure reasons for
justifying the status quo, and in success only limited
progress—the cynic whom with good cause Martha fears,
and under the welter of strictures in her "proper" marriage she almost becomes.

Apart from realities are idealities; and the discrepancy between them sustains the impetus for Martha's quest. Most positive in her thinking (and most consistent) is her desire to be free, liberated intellectually, socially, physically, politically, psychologically—and just about in that order throughout the sequence. (Curiously enough, *the* social problem of Southern Rhodesia, i.e., racism, is muted in *Children of Violence*. Africans are portrayed in shadowy outlines. Only Elias Phiri, a black government interpreter who attends the Communist meetings in *A Ripple from the Storm* and *Landlocked*, emerges full blown, but he turns out to be a company man, an informer in the pay of the white "baas," Mr. Maynard.) Indeed, through her divorce, her series of (however inadequate) lovers, her improper marriage with Anton Hesse, her connection with communism (which, too, like her other love affairs, passes through stages of flirtation, romance, disaffection, divorce), her post as "housekeeper" for Mark Coldridge, she becomes (with all attendant ironic implications) free.

Yet, Mrs. Lessing asks, to what end? Is creating oneself free, even if possible, enough? What form does it assume, what values does it possess, what changes does it assure? So-called freedom in our time has seemed little more than interchangeable with historic determinism, the metaphysical subtleties of either grossly assimilated by the violence of the century. The Marxian epigram— "Freedom is the recognition of necessity"—is no longer the stunning paradox it once was, but a self-perpetuating, self-absorbing, suicidal truth that leads through concurrent cycles to paradoxes and truths more ghastly and profound. "The idea of man creating himself," writes Hannah Arendt, "is in the tradition of Hegelian and Marxian thinking; it is the very basis of all leftist humanism. . . . But all notions have in common a rebellion against the human condition itself—nothing is more obvious than that man, be it as a member of the species or as an individual, does *not* owe his existence to himself." [4] To persist in freeing oneself, breaking from the collective, logically leads to the conclusions of Fanon and Sartre who state that "irrepressible violence . . . *is* man re-creating himself." (Italics added.) Thus, at any level, the desire for freedom leads to violence, and violence (raised to the highest level) to the potential—or, in Mrs. Lessing's fiction, the actual—extinction of man. "The practice of violence," Mrs. Arendt writes elsewhere, "like all action, changes the world, but the most probable change is a more violent world." [5]

Children of Violence nowhere pretends to political philosophy, but as a work of an informed and formidable intelligence it draws from such wellsprings of thought. What it shows is how a woman (a fictional, not a political entity) must make her personal choice and commitment within the impersonal and cosmic shifts of history and revolution.

Mrs. Lessing is never so unrealistic as to expatiate on the impossible, a moratorium on violence. While in the flush of "nonviolent idealism" Martha may tell Thomas Stern that "violence does not achieve anything," but its temper, its complexities, the abhorrent means and ends of its methods drive her, mold her reactions, and keep her fighting free of the deadened personalities surrounding her. More than a mere phenomenon, violence is integral to the human condition, a manifestation of fate, in one way even seen quasi-religiously, as the following half-ironic litany suggests:

> Martha did not believe in violence.
> Martha was the essence of violence, she had been conceived, bred, fed and reared on violence.
> Martha argued with Thomas: What use is it, Thomas, what use is violence? [6]

Its use, alas, grows clearer every year. "I am violent; therefore I am" may become the *cogito* of the twentieth century. Perhaps it is through violence alone that its children know who and what they are as they huddle under the single roof of the global village or lash out, guerrillalike, to preserve their vision of the good and beautiful from the destroyers of freedom and choice. Few of us seek violence as a way of life, yet more and more it has inescapably become the way to keep the vision intact. "Violence in a social system," Arthur Miller wrote not long after the 1968 Democratic convention in Chicago, "is the sure sign of its incapacity to express certain irrepressible needs. The violent have sprung loose from the norms available for that expression." [7] Which is another way of saying epigrammatically what Mrs. Lessing says novelistically. Needs must be reexamined; norms broken down or changed; the cycle interrupted; the distrust and suspicion of history (which may repeat itself, but so what! one must act as if it didn't in order to challenge inevitability) perpetuated.

Accepting the kinetic theory of violence and its reflex action (the need to effect change), Mrs. Lessing is nonetheless appalled by them at every turn. What she writes of the early fifties is no less valid for the middle fifties, early sixties, or so on, ad infinitum or until we explode the possibilities of reckoning time at all.

> The bad time continued. It was expressed in a number of separate events, or processes, in this or that part of the world, whose common quality was horror—and a senseless horror. To listen, to read, to watch the news of any one of these events was to submit oneself to incredulity: this barbarism, this savagery, was simply not possible. [8]

The thing is, of course, that it *is* possible, and that within such contexts the individual is unable to fare better than the world. Fear, vacillation, warping, and destruction operate as much on the personality of one as on the collective personality of billions. Martha gains little from the changes of violence she lives through and less from the limited violence of changes in her own life. The cycle of one individual creating himself moves toward a dead end, no matter that the cycle begins anew for someone else.

For Martha, then, freedom and determinism lead to change, yet both ways are narrow, both gates strait. After the rebellion of adolescence, she is attracted to the easy patterns laid out before her as the wife of the rising Douglas Knowell, intellectually a cut above the other members of the Sports Club (he reads the *New Statesman* and is therefore, to the naïve Martha, liberal and engagé); but the pact made with respectability fragments her further; more even than when she was at loose ends and indecisive. She comes to despise his lip-service liberalism, his competence, his authority, his mediocrity, and her own role as wife, then mother. Her life with Knowell—detailed in *A Proper Marriage* painfully, intimately, and at times with Lawrencean savagery—unfolds through the image of the ferris wheel at the local fun fair, illuminated and heady (her social life at the club), hypnotic and frightening (the glazed, bovid vegetating in wifedom and motherhood), and, in its starkest aspects, ultimately deterministic, symbolizing change without change. Separating from Knowell, she can only enter once more into a construct of violent and open relationships that she hopes will let her grow. Yet her growth cannot keep pace with society's disintegration. Inevitably Martha's vitality, concern, altruism seem mere ripples in the storm of selfishness and indifference; and the flotsam of her still undefined personality, drifting toward health and freedom, becomes swallowed in the mad, convulsive heavings of history.

One must naturally ask how Mrs. Lessing, who has written off the past and is balefully apocalyptic about the future, can sustain interest in the human condition at all, or hold out that feathered ephemera known as hope for the human race. Indeed, if the blow-up is coming—and at dead reckoning Mrs. Lessing gives us about twenty years grace—why bother with such lesser alternatives as expanding the means and meanings of freedom, limiting the hold of necessity, escaping the grinding of the cycle, or charting the changes within and without that will no longer leave us divisive, either as individual or collective beings?

The point is that she both cares and hopes, but has surrendered all pretense of finding the answer for us. She accepts—as her heroine comes to accept—the struggle between the individual conscience and the collective as ontogenic. Both exist and develop in terms of the other: one will always rebel, one will always attempt to absorb. This is historic; it may well be catastrophic. Mrs. Lessing has appended to the sequence future chronicles of catastrophe that seem as rationally prophetic as fictionally accurate. But she has not chosen to write a *Brave New World*, a *1984*, a *We*, or *A Clockwork Orange*, all novels of individual rebellion predicated upon ideological certainties.

Her "maps of destruction" (pieced together from sections in *The Four-Gated City*) have new coordinates, but they are almost archetypal. First comes the "stripping process," when society is like an "organism . . . unable to think, whose essential characteristic is the inability to diagnose its own condition." The controlling emotion is fear. The organism thrashes about in an attempt to protect itself, "[stunning] into immobility" anything and everything inimical to it.

The process is accomplished [Mrs. Lessing continues] . . . through words. A word or phrase is found: Communism, traitor, espionage, homosexuality, teenage violence . . . Or anger, or commitment, or satire. The organ . . . finds a word for something that threatens.

Anarchy, irresponsibility, decadence, selfishness— into this box, behind this label, gets put every kind of behaviour by which the creature is made nervous . . . Finally, the process becomes ridiculous even to the creature itself—quick, quick, a new word, a new label . . . Anything that will stop the process of thought for a time, anything to sterilise, or to make harmless: to partition off, to compartmentalise.[9]

Then comes the "rubbing-down process," when people are sucked further and more rapidly into the mechanism and machinery of fear: "fear of what other people might think; fear of being different; fear of being isolated; fear of the herd we belong to; fear of that section of the herd we belong to." [10] Eventually, individual consciences become the collective, and society is so homogenized that when the organism decays, it decays entirely.

This is a gloomy view of things. In the ten years since the writing of *The Golden Notebook* Mrs. Lessing has modified her views of human capabilities or perfectibility. There, individual salvation was conceived as an abstraction or dream but it seemed within grasp. Anna Wulf states it baldly: "I want to be able to separate in myself what is old and cyclic, the recurring history, the myth, from what is new, what I feel or think that might be new." [11] In order to be original and free, one must live in a state of subjective rebellion, alert to the specific historic milieu, alive to the immeasurable burden of keeping nihilism at bay through hope, wary of any and all actions that mechanically recapitulate the past, that force us (paraphrasing Fr. John Carey) [12] to act in a way we do not believe, to abide by principles we do not respect, to live and become like the people we detest. Though she has often remarked on the impossibility of "being" her heroines, or doing all that they have done, Mrs. Lessing obviously suffers many of their same divisions, inhabiting the penumbra between substance and shadow, shadow and act. At once hopeful of human progress, she knows that it is people, blinded by fundamental prejudices, enslaved by their sensibilities and hang-ups, bound by the past and skeptical of the future, who inhibit it.

Clearly, the answer in *The Golden Notebook* is no longer enough. It has become increasingly harder to work the act of separation Anna thought possible, perhaps because of the way Mrs. Lessing herself has changed, certainly because of the way the world has changed. Even more disastrous than the dichotomies of apocalypse envisioned by Yeats over thirty years ago—"The best lack all conviction while the worst,/Are full of passionate intensity"—is the amalgamation of best and worst. This accounts for the panic, despair, and feelings of futility Mrs. Lessing's characters share, raised to the shrillest pitch in *The Four-Gated City*.

What happened seems to be this: The postwar years immersed everyone in commitment and overconviction, while at the same time rending them apart. Impossible goals dislocated the paths of any quest. The fallings-out between Trotskyite and Stalinist, Zionist and Communist, liberal and revisionist became as much barriers to discovering the truths of self and society as the moral antagonism between white and black, superman and scapegoat. Affirmation of our collective selves caused our separation from each other as human beings, if not our actual destruction. And the separation has become more historically complete as the raw materials of ideals and ideologies have become warped into uniform, tasteless, poisonous credos. The myths that should have led us on to reform, progress, and peace have only returned us atavistically to the destructive abstraction of the myths themselves.

And so in *Children of Violence* Mrs. Lessing sets about showing, first of all, how such myths have failed. Dreams of brotherhood turn into absurd harangues over communistic and socialistic philosophies; love becomes, more often than not, hot, rapid, unsatisfactory copulation and Freudian psychologizing; psychotherapy itself, the attempt to cure neuroses and madness, becomes one more brand of madness; ultimate madness is lodged in the myth of the state, no longer concerned with self-preservation, but self-destruction. The quest for Eden or the Promised Land or the Grail is mired in the slough of stale societies and the same old political and social cycles of decay. Martha is in every way "landlocked" amidst "ists" and "isms," "ocracies" and "ologies," desperate in her desire to belong, but finding belonging increasingly impossible. Again and again Mrs. Lessing shows how the collective generates conflict between the self as subject and the self as object. Inevitably it incorporates every new idea, every new sensation into a collective idea, a collective sensation, branding, categorizing, institutionalizing.

The best illustration of this is found in the long sections treating Martha's connection with communism. Dotted with several unhappy love affairs, with a good deal of melodrama (the bourgeois tyrant Mr. Maynard trying to wrest his son's illegitimate child from the poor prole Maisie being particularly notable), but mostly with long political and ideological perorations (carried on with gusto as often in bed as at party meetings), these sections picture the decline and fall of the party in Zambesia, and undoubtedly serve as a model for the decline and fall of the party anywhere.

Mrs. Lessing's personal connections with the party aside, it is understandable that communism should occupy so much of a sequence dealing with multilevel changes. Communism is, after all, one of the great myths of our time: the god risen from the ashes of depression, revolution, and war. Yet equally true, this grandest of all myths of a collective uniting mind, body, and soul has never dissolved the older, more humanistic and natural myth of liberty, equality, fraternity. Once the flesh and bones of rebellion, communism has become (in many cases) its specter, the myth of the god that failed.

Its impact, however, has been enormous. Historically it must be reckoned as one of the most profound agents of change, a force that has opened limitless choices for millions of hopeless peoples. Nothing before it has so totally affected so much of the world. Thus when Mrs. Lessing tells of the breakup of the committed Communist group in Zambesia—a breakup brought about externally through pressures of conservative politicians and fear-mongering during the war, and internally through intriguing, backbiting, sniping, infidelities to each other and to basic beliefs—she is compressing into a moment the disintegration of a hundred years. The failure of communism, at that time, in that place, is beset with the disillusionment of historic change, and the necessity to revert to the means of personal change.

Whatever else communism may have done for Martha, it came the closest to giving her an historic sense, if not a sense of history. Wrenched from one of the few identities she has had, "cut off from everything that had fed her imagination" (the war in Europe, the plight of the Red Army, "the guerillas in China, the French Underground, and the partisans in Italy, Yugoslavia and Greece"), cut off, in short, from a cause, she imagines vistas of tedium stretching on toward no apparent oases of change. Involvement with the collective has brought about an ambiguous, far from wholly satisfactory dependency on other persons. All groups start well enough by lending us an acceptable identity (Mrs. Lessing implies) and end by usurping it entirely.

This is yet another dimension of the sequence's irony,

and, even at the level of Martha's private quest, a lesson of history. She must now explore her personality alone to see if, without benefit of the collective, she has a personality. In every way she is "landlocked" (the title of the fourth volume in the series) by her physical entrapment in Zambesia, by her mental state. She has the realization of being "locked in herself," of "sticking it out, waiting, keeping herself ready for when life would begin," and arriving at the knowledge that only she can separate the "sense of herself" from the external reality.

In *Landlocked*, Mrs. Lessing explores Martha's plunge into solipsism by way of another myth—love. Much more than an identity search, the novel is really a love story that sometimes gains the intensity and gutsy hysteria and passion of Lawrence. While in love with the farmer-intellectual, Thomas Stern, who tries absorbing her in his mission, Martha experiences some of the most penetrating changes in the series. She becomes aware of herself—her mind, psyche, being—first through another, then independently, though still not quite understanding herself. As subject, and as object, she is made part of a particular, often overbearing and repetitive love that colors her view of the world without, while working upon her identity from within. Out of this hopeless and passionate affair (as opposed to many of Martha's affairs that are hopeless and without passion) she uncovers fresh fragments of her being and fits them in place. But no more than communism can love answer for total identity. In the long run it, too, becomes another failed myth.

As does many another. Indeed, the breakdowns of these old myths are clicked off, one by one, with devestating accuracy and dissonant detachment. But in the final accounting the question is what new myths, if any, does *Children of Violence* offer instead?

After two or three volumes it is fairly clear that Mrs. Lessing believes no matter how we play at sloughing off our old skins we are forever dogged by the "hound of repetition." Freedom should not be, but somehow always is, the recognition of necessity. Martha's love affairs are continually frustrating or tragic; her men are all dreamers; in middle age she is uncomfortably like her mother; and her old self, Martha Quest, "that girl, shrill, violent, cruel, cold, using any weapon fair or foul to survive, as she had had to, as everyone's first task was to do, had been stripped off her, had gone away, was simply a character worn for a day or two, a week or two, a year, half a dozen years, by . . . anyone else who needed it." [13] Change, in other words, perpetuates recurrence: in one way, a cyclical slap-in-the-face for those who optimistically would like to view history not merely as the temporal progress of the species, but as the intellectual and spiritual progress of the individual.

There is an adjunct to this as well. As Mrs. Lessing has it, our personalities and our self-styled attempts at change more often than not seem futile placed beside cosmic continuance. No matter how much we think ourselves changing, we can never rival the immutable, nonintelligence of things that endure above and beyond us. Our life is—or should be—less a matter of yielding to the implacability of necessity than understanding its matter-of-factness. This is an affirmation in no ironic terms of our need to grow while all the while realizing our inferiority. It is what Thomas Stern tells Martha in one of their last meetings:

[I'm smaller than] that star over there, that star's got a different time scale from us. We are born under that star and make love under it and put our children to sleep under it and are buried under it. . . . Now we try all the time, day and night, to understand: that star has a different time scale, we are like midges compared to the star.[14]

And beyond "understanding," Mrs. Lessing is telling us to *do* something, for "something new is trying to get born through our thick skins." Doing and becoming are the only ways to combat what might seem hopeless and lost. Wars will go on; people will die of starvation and slaughter; holocausts have come and will come again; but there is something in the will—not necessarily indomitable, merely human—that will seek escape from the cycle of violence.

From these two premises of tension—we must simultaneously submit to and rebel from what is cyclical to the individual conscience and the collective—is born the new myth. The monumental ambivalences of the myth are no better summed up than in *The Four-Gated City*, which compresses the themes in the sequence while raising them to fever pitch. The novel is a long recapitulation of the madness that has become our age: a tangible and abstract portrait of the continuum of madness that embraces things congenital, personal, sexual, mental, scientific, political, global. Madness is the metaphor of our age, the only possible metaphor for a world gone mad. But there is another kind of madness as well that allows men like Mark Coldridge to persist in a dream of utopia, the four-gated city,

> the mythical city, the one which appeared in legends and in fables and fairy stories, and . . . a hierarchic city . . . He proceeded to describe it, as clearly as if he had lived there; and she, laughing affectionately at him, who knew this archetypal city so well yet said he believed in nothing but a recurring destruction and disorder, joined him in a long, detailed, fantastic reconstruction which, by the time they had finished, was as good as a blueprint to build.[15]

The archetypal city, built by man, destroyed by man, can only be built by man again; not in the future, but now. Mrs. Lessing has hoarded her tour de force for the eleventh hour of the series. The vision of the four-gated city goes even beyond the fiction of *Children of Violence*. It is one of an Eternal Present, the only legacy left us after the past has failed (memory fades; history lies) and the future has grown too bleak to contemplate. This vision is mirrored in Martha's last thoughts:

> She had learned that one thing, that most important thing, which was that one simply had to go on, take one step after another: this process in itself held the keys. And it was this process which would, as it had in the past, be bound to lead her around to that point where—asking continuously, softly, under one's breath, Where, What is it? How? What's next? . . . She walked beside the river . . . feeling herself as a heavy impervious insensitive lump that, like a planet doomed always to be dark on one side, had vision in front only, a myopic searchlight blind except for the tiny three-dimensional path open immediately before her eyes . . . She thought . . . Where? But *where*. How? Who? No, but *where*, where . . . Then silence and the birth of a repetition: W*here*? Here. Here?
>
> Here, where else, you fool, you poor fool, where else has it been, ever.[16]

After the faithlessness, the illusiveness, the inadequacies, and the destructiveness of everything in the century that once fed our illusions—love, intellect, religion, politics, technology, psychotherapy—we must return to that pristine starting point: here. In the end, one cannot feel that Mrs. Lessing has given up, for to give up is to give up entirely. Belief in the present, hope in the present, salvation in the present, change in the present, continuing and reviving beginnings in the present is the new myth she offers us, the last myth we can cling to, the myth we had better believe if we would escape the doom of the old myths. So long as there are those who sow violence, there will always be, alas, children to reap it, but also children who remain relentless in their quest to tame it.

2

Olivia Manning
The *Balkan Trilogy*: The Quest for Permanence

A solid, monolithic theme projects from Olivia Manning's *Balkan Trilogy* and that is "uncertainty." The series concerns itself neither with abstract or metaphysical theories of time, refashioned or shifting ideologies, nor various plays for power or status; but with the often bare, ironically conditioned facts of living in uncertainty —uncertainty not as an accident, but as a constant of life—in a world over which hangs the certainty of ruin.

Of the novel sequences at hand, Miss Manning's is the least self-conscious, the least arty, in a sense the easiest, but one of the most knowledgeable about common experience. It strives not for effects but for a single effect: to show a society teetering on, about to plunge into, an abyss, and to show people caught up in the making of history at a time when the mere debacle of the First World War was about to yield to the holocaust of the Second. Yet to show all this with something rivaling an antiepic, antiromantic sweep, to show how in this extraordinary decade the everyday world, through uncertainty, runs down.

For most of the trilogy Miss Manning's extraordinary world is Bucharest during the early years of the war, a city crammed with its complement of adventurers, expatriates, emigrés, opportunists, money barons, civil servants, and princes who suddenly find themselves on the threshold of history. Part comic-opera Ruritania in its feudality, its gilt and gaudiness; part political nightmare in its ferment of royalist, liberal, and fascist factions, Bucharest reflects the pretensions and tensions of a Rumania as heterogeneous as Durrell's Alexandria or Burgess's Malaya. It is a presence, a force of some magnificence before it squanders "the great fortune" (the title of the first volume in the sequence) to become "the spoilt city" (the title of the second). Pressured from within and without, part of a country neutered by its fence-sitting neutrality, ransacked of its dignity, culture, wealth, and civilization, Bucharest becomes the battleground for a kind of primal survival, and, as Miss Manning makes symbolically apparent, a Troy fallen anew.

Also, the mood of the capital, alternating between euphoria and hysteria, acts as a barometer for the fluctuations of history that counterpoint the less frenzied, but more closely woven lives of the ambassadors of the everyday world, Guy and Harriet Pringle, people ordinary without being mediocre, relevant and meaningful without being vitally important. Guy, a lecturer in English literature at the University of Bucharest, and his wife (as the series opens, bride) provide essentially opposing but complementary reactions to the confusion of the times as they try to understand life and each other under the relentless crescendo of war. Guy, "a large, comfortable, generous, embraceable figure," is free, energetic, adolescent, innocent, and, above all, idealistic; Harriet is constrained, a trifle reactionary, sensitive, logical, and realistic. In outlook the Pringles are probably more temperamentally at odds than necessary, though they neatly fulfill Miss Manning's needs as vehicles for and reflectors of change, for indeed no single *Weltanschauung* could possibly cope with such an "uncopeable" phenomenon, at that time, in that place. Their differences, however, are only means to identical ends: a fixation on a goal in

Guy's case (teaching at whatever cost), and the striving for a goal in Harriet's (independence as a wife, comrade, woman). Both seek stabilization against the winds of change blowing hither and yon. It is precisely Harriet's growth in the series (her progress from an intransigent realism in her view of the world and of Guy, to an understanding that "to have one thing permanent in life as they knew it was as much as they could expect"), and the chastening of Guy's selfish idealism, that make the novels so personal a statement on the laboring for continuity in the face of change.

Yet, though the pull of the *Balkan Trilogy* is toward poles of order, Miss Manning questions persistently the need for questing after permanence at times of drastic flux. Indeed, the idea that survival is to be valued in and for itself submits to its own self-irony. Undoubtedly for this reason the author (at points in the series) overshadows hero and heroine with her one true original, Prince Yakimov, part pander, part cad, part Pagliaccio, whose overcoat ("given m'Dad by the Czar") is as much symbol as poignant cliché of the aristocrat's ill fortunes between wars, as, say, Widmerpool's "good sensible shoes" and *his* overcoat are symbolic of the plodding, rising parvenus in *The Music of Time*. "Poor, old Yaki"—an epithet for himself implying not only poverty but effeteness—becomes from the beginning an incarnation of the temper of the times: expedient, vacillating, shifting, and amoral. His rise and fall are interwoven with the fate of the Pringles. As they move toward their own feeling of what is permanent in life and endure, seeking permanence as a ballast in the sea of change, he founders and goes under. Yaki becomes the victim of uncertainty; the Pringles (in however limited a sense) become victors over it.

The note of uncertainty is struck in the first volume and the changes rung on the themes of wealth and fortune. "Rumania," the economist Klein tells the Pringles, "is like a foolish person who has inherited a great fortune. It is all dissipated in vulgar nonsense." [1] In one way this is quite true. The madcap displays of fading opulence, the *fin d'empire* parties, petty corruption, and blackmail abound. Again, from the beggars of Bucharest who infest the city like cankers, from the beggary of Yaki who lives for the day the monthly remittance puts in his hands a "bit of the ready," to the expropriation of funds by the king and his toppling dynasty, to the once powerful Jewish banker, Emanuel Drucker, stripped first of his wealth, then his life in a preview of Fascist pogroms that were to become a banality of holocaust, Miss Manning presents the continuum of wealth. Everything becomes part of the high-level charades depicting Rumania's attraction into the Nazi orbit, the "nonsense" that changes the magnificent city into a shabby, decadent, gilt-edged nightmare.

But much of the so-called nonsense revolves about the mere means of survival. Fortune, to Yaki, an improvident, ridiculous vestige of the older order, is living a hand-to-mouth existence as he shuffles from one capital to another. For Harriet (arriving in Budapest with Yaki at the opening of the trilogy), fortune is something other than living at subsistence level, but something nearly as precarious. Though the wife of a man accepted by the Rumanians because he is an Englishman and therefore an "ally," and valued by the "organization" and his students, Harriet is (and for much of the sequence remains) an outsider in the country and in Guy's circles. Like Yaki, she too is an exile.

But in the widest sense, these shifts of fortune crystallize the uncertainty principle upon which, for Miss Manning, history is based, and into which fit the day-to-day patterns of life. Each volume in the trilogy is divided into four sections, and all sections are headed by a concrete noun that sets the central historic event, the background against which the characters act out their reactions to change. In *The Great Fortune*, for example, "The Assassination" concerns the murder of the pro-British prime minister, Calinescu, the suppression of the élitist Iron Guard (a Fascist group founded by the charismatic Codreanu), and the installation of the blood-and-thunder premier, Ionescu; "The Centre of Things" presents an intimate "at home" with the Druckers—a privileged insight into the psyche and society of a wealthy Jewish family that lives in disbelief and fear at their persecution; "Snow" shows the winter before the amnesty of the Iron Guard; "The Fall of Troy" parallels the fall of Paris. Throughout, Harriet is at the center of things, growing as Rumania (and the rest of Europe) decline and fall, charting her own change and the change of others, becoming involved with the "permanent life" of the place—a permanency that is really the permanency of instability.

In one way Harriet is not unlike Mann's Hans Castorp, whose stay on the magic mountain consists for the most part in "getting used to not getting used." Uncertainty begins as an emotional response to the physical condition before it is taken as the condition itself. Arriving in Bucharest from relatively fixed circumstances of life in England—it is still 1938—she finds herself ill suited to enter either into Guy's professional or social life. At times, in fact, she is thoughtlessly, though never maliciously, excluded by him, and consequently represses any intimacy with his friends (male or female) or with favored students. Her only refuge is a growing friendship with one of Guy's more sober, pessimistic colleagues, Clarence Lawson, and with Bella Nicolescu, an Englishwoman married to a Rumanian.

Harriet, a staunch realist but scarcely a tower of strength, moves between depression and confusion in searching for some niche in the disintegrating society of Bucharest during the "phoney war." Miss Manning's flat, unequivocal naturalism is generally successful at capturing the ambience that makes Harriet's uncertainty viable as she strives somehow to put out tendrils, then shaky roots. But watching her grow is at first a dispiriting business. For one thing, it is never quite clear what she originally grew from, the spadework necessary prior to planting whatever she may eventually grow into. For another, her change in the face of change is really best accomplished after she gravitates away from the simple emotionalism of introspection or "response"—after, that is, she becomes less internal and passive and begins contact with the life about her.

An instance of the former condition (which one would not want too much of) occurs early in the first volume. Harriet, exposed but a short time to the frayed nerves and interrupted heartbeat of Bucharest, and in a rare attempt at intellectual rapprochement with Guy, comments on the political situation. Rumania, at this point, is not so much neutral as a shuttlecock between Germany and Russia.

> "Wherever one is," she said, "the only thing certain is that nothing is certain."
>
> Guy looked surprised. "There are several things of which I am completely certain," he said. . . . Among [others]: that freedom is the knowledge of necessity; and there is no wealth but life. When you understand that, you understand everything."
>
> "Even the universe? Even eternity?"
>
> "They're unimportant."
>
> "I think they're important. . . . Imagine the possibilities of eternity. This life is limited, whatever you do with it. It can only end in death."
>
> ". . . . I am not interested in eternity. Our responsibilities are here and now." [2]

All this is a bit heady. No character comes to life through epigrams. Of course Miss Manning's design is clear; the irony is self-evident. But in order to catch something of her heroine's profound feelings and obvious naïveté, she runs the risk of two-dimensionalizing her. Harriet, a pre-molded bundle of psyche and intelligence, is in danger of becoming static. She only truly begins to grow when she leaves off bothering with the cosmic and directs attention to life. Her dissatisfaction with Guy's ex-girl friend's always hanging about, her discomfort at the home of the Druckers, her aversion to Yaki who puts the bite on her when occasion arises—all, to be sure, low-level problems compared to thoughts of the universe—are the best preparation for later reversals and for crises of life and death. As she reflects later on, "for her, and for Clarence, life was an involute process: they reserved themselves—and for what? With Guy it was a matter to be lived." [3]

The distinction, quite simply, is between thinking about life and doing something (anything) with it, and Harriet is never certain which of the two games to play. Respecting Guy, loving him, even at times "[following] in his wake," she is drawn toward his hyperactive life of action that lacks serious accomplishment, of intellectual stimulation without serious thought. Being, however, her own woman, she is also led into feeling that living for the unexpected, crowding life with a great deal of busy, fussy things cannot enrich or fulfill for very long. Continual change becomes as valueless and as meaningless as no change at all. But no sooner does she partially adjust to the permanence of impermanence with something of stoic resolution, than she finds herself more alone than before. Like Rumania, she is still sitting between two stools.

Harriet is exiled to the north of loneliness in the last section of *The Great Fortune,* primarily concerned with Guy's amateur production of *Troilus and Cressida.* More than marking his character, Guy's hobbyhorse for producing theatricals reflects his perpetual engagement in escapist pursuits. The play itself counterpoises Trojan and Greek with members of the English colony and its contingent of Rumanian adherents, creating an apt (if at times contrived) parallel with those who have played roles in the "fall" of Bucharest. The play holds up a mirror to a mirror. It is a stunning conceit of Miss Manning's, embracing at once the three significant spheres of action in *The Great Fortune*: the real-life drama of the actors; the interplay between Rumanian and European history; and the fickleness, reversals, and insecurity brought about by all wars. The humdrum conflicts of daily life mesh with the imperative conflicts of a society verging on chaos. The actual present becomes both universal and mythic.

For a moment Miss Manning captures a timeless suspension between myth and reality that defies the changes slowly being ground out of the war machine. The outside world (evacuation at Dunkirk; the invasion of Norway, Sweden, and Denmark; a France about to capitulate) is forgotten in the exuberance of rehearsals as the characters live their classic, appropriate roles: Sophie Oresanu (Guy's old flame) as Cressida; Inchcape, the head of the English department at the university, as Ulysses; Yaki, the "social pander of all ages," as Pander; Dubedat (of considerable importance later on) as Thersites. Harriet, significantly enough, is uncast, and can act as something of an observer; in fact, a kind of Cassandra.

Harriet stared up at Guy, her heart melting painfully in her breast, and asked herself what it was for—this expense of energy and creative spirit. To produce an amateur play that would fill the theatre for one afternoon and one evening and be forgotten in a week. She knew she could never give herself to such an ephemeral thing. If she had her way, she would seize on Guy and canalise his zeal to make a mark on eternity. But he was a man born to expend himself like a whirlwind.[4]

The fall of Paris, marking the conclusion of *The Great Fortune*, is the cold shower of reality for the actors, who, "like travellers unwillingly returned from brilliant realms, not adjusted to their return," must surrender their mythic masks. And despite Harriet's reaffirmation of Guy's earlier belief—"The great fortune is life. We must preserve it"—a feeling that decadence permeates survival overrides all else.

This is supported in *The Spoilt City*, dramatically the apex of the trilogy, being most fully descriptive of the decadence that sets in after disintegration. History courses toward "revolution, man's occupation by the enemy." The belly of the Trojan horse is about to open. Here, more than elsewhere, the theme of uncertainty parallels the flux of history, and the novel is rich with pictures of the change. It is 1940. Rumania has been steadily ceding territory on the demands of Russia; she is shortly to lose Bessarabia and Transylvania. The change in the atmosphere of Bucharest is radical as "thousands of people [wander] the streets as though waiting for a sign that their disorganized world would become normal again."[5] Tremors of an earthquake image the quite literal, more potent quake of the Iron Guard, restored to full power, and the dead, once-reviled Codreanu, now elevated to something of a deity. The tinkling, irresponsible laughter of the cafés is drowned, then stilled by the drill of the Guardists boots; the music of the nightclubs yields to repeated and discordant chants of "Capitanul" ("the Captain"), the theme song of the Guards that come to strike at first irritation, then incredulity, and at last, for some, terror.

There are, too, the overall changes of the circumstances of the country. In a remarkably sustained and energetic section (perhaps the best in the sequence), Miss Manning charts Yaki's round trip from Bucharest to Cluj, where (in order to pick up a bit of the ready) he has gone under auspices of a British wire service. The train ride is a kind of thematic springboard for the rising war fever; one leaps from the particular to the universal. In a way the harried, stuffy monotonous ride to Cluj dismally contrasts with the journey opening *The Great Fortune*, filled with expectation and promise. More telling, though, and more harrowing is Yaki's terrifying wait for the return train to Bucharest, the desperation at the crowded Cluj station of all those waiting to flee from revolution and the tentacles of the swastika. The train itself becomes a symbol of escape and terror.

But it is personal change—starker and more apprehensive—that is again at the center of *The Spoilt City*. Sasha Drucker, the son of Emanuel Drucker and one of Guy's prize students, who once struck Harriet as "some nervous animal grown meek in captivity," reappears "[smelling] of the grave," forced, because of a rash of Jew-baiting, into hiding at the Pringles. Nor do the favored fare better than the scapegoats. "This is not an aristocrat's war," Yaki's old friend and Gauleiter of Cluj, Count Freddi, tells him. Yaki, a mouse in the lion's den, taking brandy at his leisure, and the flaccid, jaded Count Freddi, bolstered by the fortunes of war, are pictures of aristocratic indolence and luxury respectively, but they also offer a tough-minded look at selling-out, the decisive recognition by Miss Manning that the aristocratic sun has gone under.

In war, however, the repatriated are but second cousins to the expatriated. Expedience becomes the keynote of existence. Inchcape, a sick and broken Ulysses after being roughed up by the Iron Guard, holds that the "important thing is to survive"; Bella, because she can pass for a Rumanian, grows distant and patronizing to Harriet; Clarence Lawson, more whining, petulant, sorry for himself, leaves; and the volatile Toby Lush and dour Dubedat (a pair as comically insidious as Rosenkrantz and Guildenstern) bolt, like Yaki, for Athens when the king abdicates under the Guardist take-over and new revolutionary government.

Despite the situation dictating expediency, Guy and Harriet hang on, as much from habit as from the realization that war precludes many varieties of action or reaction that are found in normal patterns of living. Everything comes down to the grubby matter of survival: whether to turn out the prying Yaki who is sniffing about trying to uncover Sasha's identity; whether to continue at the university, leave Bucharest, return to England. All choices are sports of chance and uncertainty. Their course, Harriet notes, lies between desperation and desperation. For Europe at large, the despoiling of Rumania —"spoiled" suggestive of taint and slow-spreading stain —means one more neutral cog engaging itself in the machinery of Nazism; for the Pringles it means the defection and loss of "friends," the actual breakup of their society, the widening of the rift between them, and their separation after a spiritual stock-taking.

It is Harriet, "[keeping] dangers in view so they might not come on her unawares," who best understands that life, though caught up in the realities of danger, is not all danger. Human beings are saved by a natural ambivalence (Miss Manning implies) that lets them adjust to desperation by making each private, unimportant act— unimportant when set beside cataclysms—seem important. A sense of humanity seems to be the survival factor. Even on the "verge of confusion" one peers as easily into the clear ether of life's comedy as into the murkiness of its indignity and selfishness. Revolution crashing about them, Guy can still prepare never-to-be-given lectures, or Harriet can, with Sasha, "[sit] on the balcony exchanging nonsense rhymes, playing paper games, telling ridiculous jokes, and giggling together as helplessly as children." [6]

Like Powell, Miss Manning focuses on the trivial because in living, we do also. Like him, too, she juxtaposes the trifling and the momentous to comment on the absurdity of the human condition. Yet trivia is never expanded—as in the prolonged farces of Evelyn Waugh, say—but contracted into two faces of the human condition: the personal and the historic.

There is, in *The Spoilt City*, the briefest of scenes, slight but utterly complete. It concerns the fatuous, pompous, foppish Lord Pinkrose who, through a prize blunder of the educational organization, has been flown into a revolution-wracked city in order to give a series of memorial lectures on the English Romantics. Inconvenienced in his accommodations and the Spartan fare Bucharest has to offer, Pinkrose finds himself fobbed off on the Pringles (royal balls and parties never having materialized), sitting in their flat sipping ersatz Madeira and being harangued by Guy on the virtues of modern poetry:

> Guy leapt at once to the defense of the poets of his generation and while he talked, he refilled Pinkrose's glass. Too preoccupied and short-sighted to see when it was full, he went on pouring until the madeira ran from the table and dripped on to Pinkrose who tutted in exasperation. Full of apologies, Guy began to scrub Pinkrose's trousers and Pinkrose, tutting again, moved his legs away. [7]

The scene catches perfectly the gestures made to preserve the decorum of a society in little, an island of apology in a sea of tension. Guy and Pinkrose are safe, but trapped in their exclusive, sheltered worlds. This—the preservation of finicky form when all form is breaking down—is the pith of Miss Manning's mannered tragicomedy of manners, ironically fleshed out later at the concert. At last Pinkrose is allowed a glimpse of Bucharest's swank and glitter; it is a parade of wealth, high fashion, regalness. Only everything is wrong. Guy, by way of committing a splendid gaffe, has purchased tickets for a German propaganda concert, and humiliation is redoubled when, being the only English present, they are laughed from the hall.

The increasing frequency in *The Spoilt City* of the kind of scene that fulfills the personal drama is also an enlargement—without exaggeration—of the breaking down of the expectations and ideals of the Pringles. Harriet, learning to adjust to the flow of reversals that has no corresponding ebb, gains a perspective on Guy, and gains, too, an historic sense, realizing that life is more and more a contradiction of ideals, no matter how realistic they may seem. Yet unlike her friends, she cannot retreat into programs of communism, fascism, fence-sitting, expedience, or revolutionary-ism. Like Mrs. Lessing's heroine she must remain questing, but always uncommitted, always volatile.

The natural contrast between herself and Guy is more sharply defined. As much as she "never lets reality out of sight," Guy "keeps it at bay"; as much as she grows more interested in people for themselves, she sees that his interest in great problems is a "lack of fundamental interest in the individual"; as much as she meets truth head-on, Guy "pretends to ignore it"; and as much as he believes in "Western culture and democratic ideals," she can understand that idealism is a living thing, not an historic or isolated phenomenon, that it is equally concerned with the reality of the moment, and is not an abstraction to be embodied in a character, shouted as a creed, or embalmed as a philosophy. It is an extension of all these that causes her—in this novel of revolution—to abandon old beliefs, to defect from liberal spoutings, and to be near fatally lured into the idealism that is the spirit and heart and life of the city:

> Codreanu was an immortal. Even now his spirit was moving through the land, regathering forces . . . inspiring . . . exhorting . . . leading . . . and so on. . . . Guy, seeing the Guardists groups pushing through the streets, had said: "How rapidly they are gathering in their kind: the hopeless, the inadequate, the brute." And yet, she thought, they were the only people in this spoilt city whose ideals rose above money, food and sex. Why should the brute not be infused with ideals, the hopeless given hope, the inadequate strength? [8]

In one way this question is the most important in the trilogy, acknowledging as it does the reason why the common and unusual break down together. Time seems capable of producing an affirmative answer to Harriet's question. Cities—call them Troy, Athens, Bucharest, Paris, or Saigon—must be continually despoiled. But if so then there must be a truce, if not among nations, then with history, and the sober recognition that in order for the individual to survive, history must be seen as an end in itself, as a collection of ordered, passing events. ("You let them pass and they lose their importance," says Harriet, naïvely but accurately.) For it is the individual, however small, however indiscernible, however lost in the great plan of time, who looms most importantly. One believes again and again—despite history or because of it—that bruteness, weakness, hopelessness is not inchoate in us, that the individual can, will, must remain stable, predictable, and human within the continuum of drastic change.

On something of this note Miss Manning ends her series, winnowing from history the chaff of change. The dichotomy implicit in the very title of the final volume —*Friends and Heroes*—is the antinomy central to Miss Manning's thesis, establishing at the same time a dualism that departs from the strict monism dealt with previously. We see the forces of disintegration and reintegration interwoven, and sense that Miss Manning is attempting if not a coherent way out of the dilemma, at least a blunting of its horns. However they are to bring it off, people must create a bridge linking past, present, and future—and the future for anyone in 1940 was at best bleak—and must raise the span necessary to connect the personal and historic.

Living under impermanence hews out new attitudes and sensibilities, makes one acutely aware of choices and responsibilities as living routinely does not. Time, always a kind of arbitrary background, appears more relentless in forcing relationships, thrusting one into choices. This Harriet realizes at one point in her abortive attempt at an affair with the dashing, Byronic Charles Warden.

> He was a different order of being. His function was not to preserve his own life but protect the lives of others. In this present situation he might run no greater risk than she herself; he was not more likely to lose his life—and yet, against reason, glancing sideways in the twilight, she saw him poetic, transfigured, like one of those sacrificial youths of the last war whose portraits had haunted her childhood. With his unmarred, ideal looks, he was not intended for life. It was not his part to survive. She was required to live but he was a romantic figure, marked down for death.[9]

Here is the human flaw in the metamorphic extrusion called history: the division into heroes and friends—those who, reserved for fate and absorbed into larger dimensions of time, go on to make history; and those others who share the daily stages of change, who have no notable destiny, but, forever aspiring, forever beginning anew, creep on with time.

Beginning again in *Friends and Heroes* is, for Guy and Harriet, nearly as optimistic as in *The Great Fortune*. Together in the "indolent sunshine" of Athens, "where the fate of Rumania was a minor fracas, too far away to mean anything," they can reintegrate. All the whirled-off pieces of their lives come back like filings to a magnet. But the sense of security is not only false, it is undermining, even more so than before because they are now compelled to draw conclusions from the past which is not, as Harriet has imagined, easy to let pass.

Friends and Heroes also adds a new dimension to the trilogy. History no longer serves exclusively as the backdrop against which personal dramas are played, but is more intimately connected with them. The novel, covering a single year, is historically concerned with the fortunes of Greece, at first victorious over Italy, then defeated by her, and at the last steeling herself for invasion by Germany. Parallels to the human condition are not far from the mark. In "The Antagonists," for example, Greeks and Italians face off for a bitter campaign, as Guy, jobless, pits himself against Lush and Dubedat who try keeping him from a post at the university in Athens; in "The Victors," Greece's whittled-down forces hold back (Thermopolae-like) the Italians, as Guy and Harriet overcome their own odds by becoming absorbed in Athenian life and embarking on saving projects. The most complicated section of the entire trilogy, "The Romantics," gathers together simultaneous views of the problems already encountered, and investigates the romantic attitude toward life; the direct clash of the idealist and realist takes place on neutral grounds. Greece, euphoric at her victories, is momentarily deluded into believing she can repel the forces of the Hitler-Mussolini entente. Similarly Miss Manning investigates the romantic attitudes and relationships of Harriet, Guy, and Charles Warden, defining a view of the world that is to each acceptable, and then redefining it, opening it up to another view, in other terms, so that it may be challenged. And "The Funeral," a farewell to Yaki, shot by a security guard while unwittingly lighting a cigarette during a blackout, is also a dirge for the Balkans—Greece is the last country there to fall—and for Europe.

Crystallizing what has gone before—that is Miss Manning's purpose in this last novel. Harriet is now quite obviously the heroine, Guy less the hero, for she possesses awareness without confusion. Having taken the measure of Guy, having gotten to know her strengths and limitations, she has fulfilled her role as a persona and as a character. Harriet, of all the characters in the trilogy, comes out on top because she has done more than survive the uncertainty of life and the tragedy that ensues from that uncertainty. She has not been trapped by her ego or good intentions or the solipsism of self alone, but has risen to heights of sensitivity and responsibility, has gained (in Iris Murdoch's words) a "sense of the other."

The novel is at its best in showing Harriet's unfolding and maturing, and actually "works" through radical shifts or displacement of earlier relationships. Harriet, though early alerted to the potentialities of people, continued to think of them as relating to herself or Guy. Now she sees them as they are, not how they might or should be. The prominent weight of reversals in *Friends and Heroes* (once again accountable to the fortunes of war) are balanced by the reactions they draw from her, and act as a measure of her change. Aversion for Yaki is transformed into a mutual bond tied out of fear and sympathy. And somehow by this closeness with Harriet,

Yaki is made more human, less the ludicrous figure come onstage to wring the last note of pathos from a stock situation—the death of the fool. On the other hand an older friend, Sasha Drucker, released by the Rumanian government after waiving all rights to his father's expropriated funds, is now cool, almost hostile to the Pringles, imagining they have betrayed him by divulging his sanctuary in Bucharest. But through contact with Harriet, he, too, becomes more than the displaced Jew, no longer a stereotype but a frightened, hunted, confused youth growing to manhood.

There is, too, in Harriet, something of the tigress in abeyance—would that more of it showed!—in her scrapes with Lush and Dubedat as she fights for Guy; something of the individualist in her refusal to be indoctrinated by Guy's acquaintance, Ben Phipps, an ideological Communist and blowhard; and something of the disciple in her devotion to the eccentric Alan Frewen, part-time information officer and part-time scholar-gypsy—a relationship, in fact, easier to understand and accept than that with Charles Warden. Clarence Lawson, yet another ambassador from the past, a victim of a brief, disastrous marriage with Sophie Oresanu, also turns up, but no longer as an influence, no longer for Harriet the sane voice of cynicism in a world grown unbelievable and nightmarish.

Out of the barrenness and fear of war that gnaws at her characters, Miss Manning turns one aspect of uncertainty into partial conclusiveness. This is the relationship between Guy and Harriet, one of the major threads of the trilogy, often hard to unravel and often lost in the rich fabric of external events in Bucharest and Athens. It is with Guy, after all, that Harriet seems fated to live, not with awe but with understanding. No man is a hero to his valet or his wife; and Harriet discovers Guy's weaknesses (as well as her own) only to accept them. Alerted to the change in others, she can see Guy in a much clearer light. He turns in her eyes from saint and hero to what one knows he has been all along, a well-meaning but selfish idealist—selfish because it is really himself that he has pleased in his grand, ephemeral projects. Yet as he loses for Harriet his heroic substance, he gains substantially in other ways, though her recognition of this comes about slowly.

The Pringles' marriage wavers toward some ultimate definition in *Friends and Heroes*. Guy, "not to be shut up in intimacy has the world for his chief relationship, [not] really understanding any other." [10] It is a fact Harriet cannot readily accept at first. Losing Guy to his socialist cronies and café revolutionaries contributes to her collapse in Athens, but her recovery (and increasing resiliency) takes her further than any previous minor rebuffs toward a world outlook.

Harriet changes, most demonstrably in her unsatisfying alliance with Charles Warden. One might with all reasonableness consider Harriet a bitch in this romantic interlude; she leads on Warden, then cuts him off. But Miss Manning is taking a hard, dim, antiromantic view of things. Wartime romance, popularized in slick fiction and films, is stood on its head. Harriet is still young—she is only twenty-one—and inexperienced in love; but she has insight enough to realize that any affair of the heart born of the impermanence of the times, is impermanent and unreal. Warden, a "romantic," need not understand life; in this respect he is like Guy. But to Harriet adultery would solve none of her problems; she would still be operating under similar conditions of impermanence. Whether in her genuine affection for Guy or her flirtation with Warden, she feels she is "not living but being fobbed off with an imitation of life," and neither love nor romance would seem to have much place in the scheme of things as they are.

Harriet does make her pact with Guy, not out of pride, neglect, or self-pity, but through grasping and voicing his fallibilities. This pact is the maturation of Miss Manning's heroine. In refusing to acquiesce in Clarence Lawson's praise of Guy as someone beyond and above them, she acknowledges at last that he is human. Life becomes significant (or should become significant) for people in terms of what they have. It is because of impermanence that Harriet loses Sasha, Charles, and her other friends, and it is to Guy she turns, not because she must settle for *anything* (and Guy is no bargain per se), but because "whatever his faults, he [possesses] the virtue of permanence." This, in a world of uncertainty, is about all one can expect.

What Harriet is left with in the end, is the reality of circumstances accruing from her years in Bucharest and Athens, the summation of the "facts of life," and Guy as the sole remaining prop. In a most conclusive way the repeated breakdown of things for the Pringles—the breakdown of the Balkans, the breakdown of the Pringles's old values, of their dependency on others, of "illusion and disillusion"—is actually the dismantling of any notion that "romance," in the sense of happy means and happy endings, might control life. What does control life is the antiromantic, the unexpected and uncertain, which, in Miss Manning's trilogy, are forced to a higher exponent. Living in *any* way during wartime can only be a postponement of life as we might know it. Perhaps in no other situation of comparable intensity and involvement are appearances so identical with reality. Life *is* what it is!

As is death. Yaki's fatal shooting is less gratuitous in the weird scheme of a world operating under war than the *actes gratuits* of other modern novelists who kill off their protagonists without so much as a by-your-leave. Miss Manning seems indeed faithful to the historic moment—as Durrell, say, has little or no respect for it at all —and is not interested in pulling rabbits out of hats. Reversals or the "suddenness of things" are not intended to beef up the limited action. (If one is not in sympathy with Miss Manning's characters to begin with, even action will never satisfy.) Rather, the tissue of change connecting life and death is built leisurely, faithfully, organically. Ideally, change overrides chance and seeks to stabilize the impermanent through the permanent; but in the *Balkan Trilogy* we see impermanence become a way of life and death in itself. Things are turned topsy-turvy. Illusion becomes disillusion, friends are taken for heroes, enemies for friends. War, producing "anxiety instead of expectation, exhaustion instead of profit," giving rise to "insecurity and fear," is real; life is not. In simplest terms war is life, just as Harriet says.

The implications here are perhaps the most unique to be found among the contemporary novel sequences. Change becomes the unexpected, chance the expected; and any romantic vision that would see otherwise is accountable to the darker truths of reality. As Miss Manning suggests, romantics—and both Guy and Harriet are romantics of the older order—are lost in this century; modern history and war have effectively annihilated any saving sense of permanence we might have once possessed. But, as Mary McCarthy has written, "the quest for certainty is itself a hero's goal," a paradoxical, testy, incontestable notion that is supported again and again by Miss Manning's trilogy. Guy and Harriet's experience is the extension of the finite into the infinite. Their fate is evanescent, but typical of those who passed nearly a decade of the twentieth century living in uncertainty. To be sure, as the sequence closes, one scarcely gives a second thought to the Pringles. No longer fictional, they are no longer historic. But while in the foreground Guy and Harriet, nonheroic heroes consigned to the world of "friends"—a world capricious, absurd, often meaningless, forever changing, forever uncertain—loom as large and important as history itself.

3

Lawrence Durrell
The *Alexandria Quartet*: Art and the Changing Vision

The *Alexandria Quartet* is easily one of the best works of the past decade. The city it evokes is exotic, vibrant, sensual, and fluid. Its characters are diverse, many quite actually "round," most symbolically relevant. Its imagery is directed toward some splendid effects; its multiple and multileveled narrative toward creating memorable (in places notorious) scenes; its sweep is broad; and, above all, it is most ambitious in its attempt to get at one of the great archetypal literary and philosophical problems: namely, the nature of love and art and the erosion of both by time and change. In every way Lawrence Durrell has written the modern, rather than merely contemporary, novel.

The temptation, however, to read it in a certain way —as a technical and pyrotechnical tour de force—is still around even after ten years, and suggests something of its limitations. For the *Quartet* is not, despite a plethora of characters, a novel of character; it is not, despite a show of polymathic learning, a novel of ideas; it is not, for all the shadow play of narrative devices, a novel of complex plot or action. It may be pretty much as the poet Ludwig Pursewarden says about his own projected novel, "nothing very *recherché* . . . just an ordinary Girl Meets Boy story"—save that the "girls" are neurasthenics, lesbians, or prostitutes suffering from nympho-, narco-, or autolepsy, and the "boys" either writers or revolutionaries (or both) suffering from an overdose of logorrhea; and the "story" alternately serves as parody, poetry, epic, whodunit, myth, and morality. Actually, the *Quartet* offers scant illumination on anything not part of its insulated hermetic world. Somewhere within the peripheries of its diffuse narratives and its lush atmosphere is, one suspects, a hub of meaning from which all else radiates. Yet again and again the center eludes us, and the sequence seems too specifically, too purely one of form, of art: a law unto itself, and a law still uncodified.

Durrell sustains any ambiguities about his work by writing (in the note to *Balthazar*) that the *Quartet* is "a four-decker novel whose form is based on the relativity proposition . . . three sides of space and one of time [constituting] the soup-mix recipe of a continuum." And critical amplifications of its major motifs—"the investigation of modern love," the portrait of the artist, the quest for wholeness, the end of romanticism, the recreation of myth, and so forth—have only further clinched the idea that with so many dangling, unintegrated, and unresolved ingredients what we have is more a soup-mix than even the author himself anticipated. For while the *Quartet* may be concerned with all these things, and while it may indeed be grounded on the theory of relativity, what it is about has seemed separable, if not at odds, with what it is. To say it is flawed as a brilliant gem is flawed is probably not enough. The flaw is integral to the gem. The question remains: Are Durrell's themes integral to his novel's form? Can one find, that is, the controlling center of the *Quartet* where they fuse?

Critiques of the novel owe much less to Durrell's notes than to the ideas culled from the overripe epigrams, aphorisms, dialogues and monologues on art and life as they issue from Pursewarden. Reduced to two statements, the touchstones for the methodology of the *Quartet* seem to be these. First:

> We live . . . lives based on selected fictions. Our view of reality is conditioned by our position in space and time—not by our personalities as we like to think. Thus every interpretation is based upon a unique position. Two paces west and the whole picture is changed.[1]

And toward the end of the sequence:

> [You] might try a four-card trick in the form of a novel; passing a common axis through four stories, say, and dedicating each to one of the four winds of heaven. A continuum, forsooth, embodying not a *temps retrouvé* but a *temps délivré*. The curvature of space itself would give you stereoscopic narrative while human personality seen across a continuum would perhaps become prismatic? . . . I can imagine a form which, if satisfied, might raise in human terms the problem of causality or indeterminacy. . . . tackled in this way you would not, like most of your contemporaries, be drowsily cutting along a dotted line! [2]

The former of these reflections is not, to be sure, terribly new. Positioning in time and space has been practiced by Jane Austen, George Eliot, and Henry James, and it is doubtful whether Durrell achieves more subtlety of effect through his many narrative devices than they through their conventional use of a reflector or an omniscient narrator. The latter musing, however, is more plastic, more original, and in a crucial way an outcropping of the first. Pursewarden is proclaiming the real problem of *any* work of fiction—the matter of getting at the traditional, raw materials of art and molding them into a distinctive and individual form. The logic of conception is often at variance with the complexities of optics—or, in this case, stereoptics—and the divergent procedures are probably apparent. The game of the realist is that of turning "selected fictions" into realities, and of a writer like Durrell, of heightening such selected fictions as already exist.

It is this last that the *Quartet* sets out to do. Life, never art but eventually transformed into art, operates in a continuum of change. The question is really how (and if) both can be kept fluid, moving, kinetic during the process of transformation, without distorting either. For life, though it may be viewed from differing perspectives, cannot be reordered except through art. Retrospectively, the *events* of life are sequential, static, historic (Pursewarden's "causality") the *interpretations* of events (the motives involved with them, if one prefers) are alone open to reconstruction ("indeterminacy"). On such terms it seems as justifiable to write the same novel four different ways as to write four novels one way, i.e., to persist in "drowsily cutting along a dotted line." Art, therefore, not life, becomes the principal focus of the artist's changing vision.

To put it another way, Durrell is writing his own "pure novel," and in form (not necessarily spirit) the *Quartet* is closer to Gide's *Counterfeiters*, say, or Nabokov's *Ada*, than to either *Remembrance of Things Past* or *Ulysses*, both of which are rigidly structured. By the pure novel one must understand that novel in which form and content are inseparable and indiscernible, a novel inspired less by life than by art. Such a novel grows but never ends, for the actual writing of it must change during the act of creation. It writes itself, so to speak, or is continually being rewritten. Edouard in *The Counterfeiters* enters this reflection in his journal "I consider that life never presents us with anything which may not be looked upon as a fresh starting point, no less than as a termination. 'Might be continued'—these are the words with which I should like to finish my *Counterfeiters*."

The "Workpoints" appended to *Clea* attribute the same sort of open-endedness to the *Quartet*, the refusal or denial to finally contain the multifaceted stuff of art in any single, rigid structure. For Durrell, as for Gide, form and content fuse, paradoxically, by their very dissociation. If (following a classic bit of aesthetics that finds its way into "Workpoints") "a work of art is something which is more like life than life itself," then any work of art that takes art for its subject might reasonably be imagined to go even one step beyond. But how? Ultimately the question becomes one of the mechanics of perception. Instead of being asked to look at a photo, or a series of photos, one is told to look at the changing angles of the camera, the changing filters in the lenses. The concern is with the simultaneous and recurring changes of the artist and his art—and how convenient that Alexandria is the city of the pharaoh-god Proteus! Not only how a writer turns life into art, but how he turns art into a higher art is the center of the *Quartet*, seen through the city and the writers who continuously create and re-create it.

Alexandria, the filament that binds and illuminates the jigsaw pieces of the novel, is a most important part of demonstrating a theory turned into practice. "What is this city of ours?" asks Darley on the opening page of *Justine*, and answers (even though his knowledge is still a limited one) by drawing us into all its associative spatial and temporal phenomena. The sequence is a remembering of Alexandria, of a city that wears many faces and means many things, no one of which is a stronger link in the "iron chains of memory" than any other. It is, for one thing, the names—personal, magic, insidious, tragic —by which it is brought to life. Nessim, Justine, Clea, Balthazar, Pursewarden, Mountolive, Melissa, Scobie become Alexandria; and Alexandria becomes the people that live It and that It lives. The city, too, is "androgynous," inverted, combining the principles of yin and yang: dark, cold, dead, as well as light, warm, alive. It is a city evil and good, loving and lustful; the image and the mirror image. Alexandria is history: the Caesars, the Ptolemys, knowledge, wars lost and won; and it is imagination, a timeless myth surrounded by the sea of time, but subject to time's erosion.

But mostly the city is the "capital of memory . . . who clutches the raw material of her daily work," a vast storehouse of the conscious and unconscious that Durrell draws upon in the course of the sequence. The collective desires and the collective wishes of those who live in Alexandria and those who move through it are fused by Durrell in a symphonic-scientific metastasis of memory. Each section of the *Quartet* provides additional insight and material for turning disparate memories into a coherent pattern, for making the city "real." Whether one first sees Alexandria as the sensual, romantic, diseased hotbed of love that feeds Justine's passions, as the center of political intrigue for Nessim, as a sphere of influence for Mountolive, as the inspiration for the art of Darley, Pursewarden, or Clea—sees it, that is, as so many literal extensions of individual egos—one must see it finally as the symbolic locale for (in Darley's words) reordering, reworking and revealing the significant side of realities that grow more illusive as one's ideas of what reality is change.

Alexandria is, at one extreme, the solid base of the novel, and, at the other, the most palpable symbol of change. Like Proust's Paris or Combray or Balbec, Alexandria is dormant, amorphous until quickened and shaped by imagination and memory, both differing functions of a single process that for Durrell is pretty much reserved for the artist. The reality of the city—what one might think of as its "life"—remains constant; the changes it undergoes are related to a widening artistic perception and the growth of the artist who is not only changing from day to day, but is part of a changing history and changing ethos. Alexandria mirrors the changes of those who live within its unravelling mystery, but with that reversal peculiar to all mirrors. In the course of the novel the city of the imagination undergoes transformation and dissolution: the "great winepress of love" becomes (for Darley) what "it must always have been—a shabby little seaport built upon a sand-reef, a moribund and spiritless backwater," [2] although it had always contained itself ambivalently, being "princess and whore . . . the royal city and *anus mundi*." As the mystery is dulled and dissipated, as the veil is lifted from Darley's eyes, as his sense of accepting many realities grows more acute, his art gains a toughness and strength. He and Clea—the pair triumphant who write the happy ending to the *Quartet*—have, in mirrorlike reversal to the city, begun in dissolution, but through a transformation brought about by themselves are at last transfigured into artists.

Metamorphoses of character and locale—the physical flux of the city—are technically less cumbersome to handle than those metaphysical changes of artistic perspective and of art. About the former, Durrell can be literal, narratorial, scenic. (It is not surprising that the exuberant praises for the *Quartet* have consistently dwelt on his incredible powers to evoke place.) About the latter, however, he must be figurative and mythic. And as Alexandria is the mirror of the life moving in, through, and around it, the mirror itself becomes chief symbol for the metamorphosis of art, that which (to quote Wallace Stevens) renders "the metaphysical streets of the physical town."

The creative act being one of reflection, retention, conversion, the mirror—which reflects, retains, converts —projects beyond narcissism, voyeurism, or even artistic autism (the more or less set pieces of sensationalism in the *Quartet*) to that of the artistic process itself. Art, seen in this way, captures reality, and at the same time reduces the spatial-temporal relationships between image and mirror image. What one finds in the *Quartet*—and the multiform variations on the "ordinary Girl Meets Boy story," together with the shifting about of characters support the idea—is an ordering more complex than either Balthazar's "interlinear," Pursewarden's "sliding panels," Justine's "five different pictures of the same subject . . . a sort of prism-sightedness," or Darley's "quatrefoil." These are all, in a way, finite approaches to reality, ways to explain or to formulate it. Durrell tries to carry this ostensible complexity beyond any of its individual parts: to hold one double-sided mirror up to another, to hold behind both of these an additional pair, behind these four yet two more, and so on. The mirrors themselves extend into space, ad infinitum, and the images between any two of them create an infinite progression as well.

What Durrell is about here is at once the fusion and disintegration of space-time: rendering the continuing quality of life (its routine, regularity, boredom) just as one might imprison an image in a mirror, and at the same time projecting the subtle or wild fluctuations of events beyond those narrative and historic methods—the conventional modes of fiction—that demand a finite ending or cyclical return. Hence, concern with "relativity" (what has drawn much too much hullabaloo over the sequence) is more nominal than actual. Actually, the *Quartet* defines change by moving off fixed points on a space-time continuum to become (substantiating for the moment the distinction of Darley's) "a work of memory rather than imagination." Durrell does not (like Joyce or Proust) mythicize an event, but the memory of it in the mind of one artist or another. Change (interpreted by memory as well as mythicized and refined by it) can no longer be thought of as the only permanent thing, but as a shifting thing in itself. And these along with time and space, normally treated as novelistic motifs, supportive props for capturing life and art, are directed to capturing the *movement* of life and art.

In the *Quartet* such movement is both temporal and spatial: the first involved with the life of Alexandria and fostered by the principal character, the second with the whole question of art, symbolized most fully by the mirror analogy and rendered through the sequence's multilevel narration. To emphasize what may not have always appeared obvious, the "story" of the *Quartet*—that is, the accumulation of lines of action on certain fixed points of the "time-space continuum"—does not change. Clearly, certain actions can be defined and pinpointed. Justine (for whatever reasons) does sleep with Mountolive, Darley, and Pursewarden; Narouz is removed by Memlik; Scobie is apotheosized. The temporal movement is, therefore, absolute. Only the spatial can be called relative, and though more inverted—what is the attraction of art compared to the louche, extravagant, at times wildly hysterical transmutations of the characters? —is more interesting.

This may be better understood through an example found toward the end of *Justine*. The vision here is not the artist's, per se, but Nessim's, in whose mind Alexandria forms and reforms along Jungian lines, ontogenically and archetypally:

> At this time he had already begun to experience that great cycle of historical dreams which now replaced the dreams of his childhood in his mind, and into which the City now threw itself—as if at last it had found a responsive subject through which to express the collective desires, the collective wishes which informed its cultures. He would wake to see the towers and minarets printed on the . . . sky, and . . . on

them the giant footprints of the historical memory
which lies behind the recollections of individual personality, its mentor and guide: indeed, its inventor,
since man is only an extension of the spirit of place.
. . . But while the gallery of historical dreams held
the foreground of his mind the figures of his friends
and acquaintances, palpable and real, walked back-
wards and forwards among them, among the ruins of
classical Alexandria, inhabiting an amazing historical
space-time as living personages.[4]

As in other philosophical passages in the *Quartet*, the
perdurable motifs of change, space, time, memory, history, and the city are here worked into the simpler movements of isolated moments—indeed, every major character in Alexandria thinks this way at one time or another
—but merge into the overall complexity. Nessim has intimations of his and the city's avatars, yet encounters them
on a single level. He can get at things by sifting out the
"palpable and real." But by its very form the *Quartet*
suggests that the problem is not quite so simplistic; it
is the problem of the historic mind opposing the artistic
one. Nessim—a visionary—is also a revolutionary, particularly hidebound by history which the artist is free to
reject. For Durrell, art is dualistic, compounded of imagination and memory, though even here there is an
important distinction to be made. "The order of the imagination is not that of memory," Balthazar writes Darley—a statement that limits and expands the *Quartet's*
aesthetic. Imagination (fictional space-time) mediates
between history (historical space-time) and memory (artistic space-time). Ultimately every writer's job is to deliver art from history—a notion one can find as readily
in Shakespeare and Keats as in Nabokov or Proust or
Durrell—and strike the balance between imagination
and memory.

The approaches to art, the methods of art, the way into art are always the implicit subjects of the *Künstler-roman*, though the *Quartet* is not an artist's novel so much as the artists' novel. Those who have a hand in creating it—namely, Arnauti, Pursewarden, Darley, and Durrell himself—are to a greater or lesser degree concerned with this very interplay of memory and imagination as it relates to time. As Darley writes, "I began to see . . . that the real 'fiction' lay neither in Arnauti's pages nor Pursewarden's—nor even my own. It was life itself that was a fiction—we were all saying it in our different ways, each understanding it according to his nature and gift." [5] The *Quartet* does not establish any hierarchy of artists; more precisely, one understands an ordering by way of continuity, for the act of creation is continuously and differently renewing itself. Thus of the many continuums in the sequence the principal one is this continuum of writers—a continuum that transforms a novel of passion, love, sadism, espionage, and good old grand guignol into a formal, logical, classically ordered work of wholeness. The square within the circle is the image for the *Quartet*.

One must begin with Jacob Arnauti, Justine's first husband. As a person Arnauti is little more than a shadow; as a novelist only slightly more than adequate. The slim volume called *Moeurs* that is put into Darley's hands is a kind of Ur-*Justine*, containing sufficient reflections to suggest that Arnauti's view of Alexandria and the life in it is, by way of being the most imaginative, at the same time the most primitive. He writes that "real people can only exist in the imagination of an artist strong enough to contain them and give them form." He wishes to "dispense with narrative articulation," to free his drama from the burden of form, to "*set [his] book free to dream.*" [6]

Clearly Arnauti eschews realism, advocates subjectivism, and reaches tentatively toward relativism on the artist's terms, if not in terms of art itself. He preaches the idealism of creation: the ideal of the artist absorbing the characters into himself until they have no life of their own, or only such that the writer lends them. What Arnauti seems to be after—and there is too little of *Moeurs* to suggest either success or failure—is an arresting of memory and history; they are sacrificed to the imagination. Arnauti tries to create the timeless world in his novel by rejecting these two adjuncts of time. He would make his characters "all bound by time in a dimension which is not reality as we would wish it to be—but is created by the needs of the work." The configuration of Arnauti's naïve aesthetic is important for several reasons. For one, it shows how Darley—still innocent as a man, undeveloped as a writer, and subject to Durrellian irony—is smitten with the fine theories and pictures Arnauti conveys, what he calls a "graceful and accurate portrait of Alexandria . . . and its women." But it further shows an incipient method of the *Quartet*. Arnauti blanks out reality. The gap between life *action* and artistic *act* is intentionally widened. Arnauti, who sees the ultimate form in no-form, contributes a single side (a singular dimension) by providing a monolithic subjectivism from which the other writers wish to escape. Darley's tentative criticism of Arnauti (that he lacks a "sense of play—that he bears down so hard on his subject matter that style becomes subject"), and Clea's (that he seems "shallow and infected by the desire to explain everything . . . to want to contain everything within the frame of reference of a psychology or a philosophy") is a double condemnation of art for art's sake and art as morality. Arnauti, while too free, is also too much a slave to form and the single vision of creation which makes art solely a matter of imagination.

This is certainly not the case with Pursewarden: on

the one hand equally put off by art for its own sake, or art as ethics or therapy—"if . . . you take it for a thing in itself, having some sort of absolute value, or as a thesis upon something which can be paraphrased [caveat critics!] surely you miss the point" [7]—but on the other hand as obtuse and monochromatic as Arnauti. Pursewarden's theories (set down as a separate chapter half-way through *Clea*) are extracted from his notebook, "My Conversations With Brother Ass." The ass in question is Darley; the conversations are in reality a monologue; but the entire section is the *Quartet's* most sustained, cool, and ironic disquisition (tirade, rather) on art, though one is cautioned from the beginning as to what should or can be taken seriously.

Pursewarden is a maddening article, rightly made much of, but often for the wrong reasons. His cloak-and-dagger activities are surely as grotesque as his ill-starred sex life or as illusive and ill defined as his poetry. Spy manqué, *poète maudit*, Wandering Jew, or Childe Harold, Pursewarden wears the multiple faces befitting a protagonist of the *Quartet*. But whether Durrell considers him artist, aesthete, dilettante, or fraud is probably in the long run less important than how he manages to bring in Pursewarden's views on art, yet another side of the sequence.

Actually Pursewarden seldom ponders "art"; the serious question with him is the possibility of being an artist. He sees himself "disguised as an eiron," understands that to become an artist "one must shed the whole complex of egotisms which led to the choice of self-expression as the only means of growth"—an unwieldy paradox that Pursewarden dubs "The Whole Joke," and one that accounts for the range of his flippant, obscure, bitter, dubious, witty, mordant, weary, and wearying pronunciamentos. The paradox of Pursewarden is that the romanticism, humanism, cynicism, and irony compounding his character are *all* made (at one time or another) to substantiate his vision of art. "Art," he writes, "occurs at the point where a form is sincerely honored by an awakened spirit." Or: "Art's Truth's Nonentity made quite explicit." And again: "Is art simply the little white stick which is given to the blind man and by the help of which he tap tap taps along a road he cannot see but which he is certain is there?" Once again: "I see art more and more clearly as a sort of manuring of the psyche." And contrarily: "Art is the purifying factor merely. It predicates nothing. It is the handmaid of silent content, essential only to joy and to love."

What Pursewarden says about art is much less significant than the way he says it. Common to all his epigrams and apothegms is their actual, rather than their interpretable value. No matter how Pursewarden may *treat* his art—and there are few samples of his serious poetry in the *Quartet* to persuade one way or the other—he *sees* it metaphorically. He is partly in the tradition of Frank Kermode's "romantics," who extract from reality images to symbolize art, but for whom art ultimately becomes the metaphor for itself; and partly a "realist" who wishes to see things as they are, to gain a "purchase on the slippery surface of reality" enough to make the "enigmatic leap into the heraldic reality of the poetic life." This "heraldic universe," as it is referred to elsewhere, is nothing less than life itself seen (as Yeats sees his dancer or chestnut tree) objectively, yet all the while supplying metaphors for art. Pursewarden's universe comes into focus by way of imagination ("the so-called act of living is really an act of the imagination"), and history ("civilization is simply a great metaphor which describes the aspirations of the individual soul in a collective form—as perhaps a novel or a poem might do").

Left with Pursewarden's impartial but poetically unsatisfying objectivity, and Arnauti's vatic, pristine subjectivity, Darley has the job of wedding subjective and objective, and at the same time making use of "memory," which the other two have blotted out or ignored. Aided by memory he is to gain the "purchase on the slippery surface of reality," and to leap from there not into dream or metaphor, but into reality once again. Darley is to deliver time through his and others' memories, but also—to limit the Proustian implications of this sort of artistic act—by following the advice of Balthazar: "To intercalate realities . . . is the only way to be faithful to Time for at every moment in Time the possibilities are endless in their multiplicity." [8]

Realities, Darley discovers, are none other than elusive and illusive multiplicities; but never purely "illusion," things as a writer (Arnauti) would like them to be, nor "reality," things (according to Pursewarden) as they are. Cast out are the neoromantic post-Pirandellian terminologies. Instead of laboring distinctions between "illusion and reality," the art of the *Quartet* confirms how each is a coefficient of the other—cotemporal and cospatial. The spirit of place inhabits the writer as much as he inhabits it. And by the very fact of having at his fingertips most of the realities of Alexandria and its people, Darley can best work and sustain the illusion: wedding, not divorcing, them, bridging the past, present, and future—the historic, the remembered, the imagined. No less than the whole *Quartet* is proof of this, for that shifting aesthetic is ultimately the changing vision of art as found in its over eight hundred pages, and stated after some seven hundred of them by Darley when he speaks of life itself as the fiction. Phrasing theoretical paradoxes may appear simpler than executing complex techniques, but Darley's understanding of life as fiction does not exclude self-irony, opening as it does the door for the fourth authorial voice—Durrell's.

To a large extent the *Quartet* is Darley: composed,

collated, reshuffled, and woven by him. It is his "inter-
calating of realities," as he moves from Arnauti's subjective vision to Pursewarden's objective one, rejecting both
but spinning out strands and threads along the way. But
even the weaver may find himself woven. In *Mountolive*
Darley is shuttled through the warp and woof of action
over which he has little effect and no control. *Mountolive* is more or less a piece of straight nineteenth-century
naturalism, but it is a tour de force in so far as the sequence is concerned. Durrell, now the "omniscient narrator" is calling the shot. He gains his own purchase on
reality by showing how subject (Darley) can turn object;
how the gothic patina, the baroque sensibilities, the
esoterica, perversion, decadence, the permeating mythic-
ness and mirrorness of Alexandria become (through a
simple and relative shift of the artist's vision) mere bas
reliefs on the greater frieze of history; how, in short,
everyone is potentially capable of moving "out of the
orbit of human [and, in many cases, artistic] free will . . .
to find themselves shackled, bricked up by the historical
process." [9]

Mountolive casts a cold eye on history and its failure
to redeem time. Mountolive himself is the symbol of a
man "bricked up by the historical process" without the
recovering powers of memory or imagination: antiromantic, empire builder turned agent provocateur, "the
stone effigy of a dead crusader." And his crisis is twofold
once he realizes life has been lived only under the illusion
that he was free to act. Space, as well as time, defeats
him. Alexandria becomes "distasteful, burdensome, wea-
risome to his spirit"; and the image of Leila Hosnani and
the memory of their love affair (an affair that antedates
those subsequent various and chaotic sexual interchanges
in the *Quartet* and sets the pattern for them) fades, dissolves in their meeting many years later. Durrell writes,
"[Mountolive] was suddenly face to face with the mean-

ing of love and time." For men without memory or imagination, time subsumes love, negates it.

Mountolive is easily the most human, the most suffering, the most "crucified" character in the sequence. A quartet of *Mountolives* would, to be sure, run swiftly downhill in its proof of time's triumph over men. But *Mountolive* is one novel only; pivotal, albeit inconclusive. It is left to the other novels to show that while time and change may be dispiriting realities, art may redeem them, just as it redeems love, or, for that matter, anything. The changing vision of art is accomplished not only in time but because of it. The artist comes to see time logically as an adjunct of the processes of art, rather than a thing strictly imperative that must be obeyed (history) or a thing mysterious that must never be understood. One might say that there is the implicit personalization of time in the sequence as well as the more obvious mythification, and only when Darley reaches one by way of the other can he truly understand the work as being "the old story of an artist coming of age." Only then can he write the mythic phrase "Once upon a time" and feel (in the words of the *Quartet's* final sentence) "that the universe had given [him] a nudge"; only then can he feel the complicity, that is, of cosmics—art, time, and space.

Like all aspirants Darley begins in blindness and error. In *Justine* he swathes time in the classical, mythic cliché of the sea—immense, formless, irrecoverable. He confronts what to all appearances is immovable and unchangeable, finding his spirit overwhelmed because he cannot enter into the space-time continuum nor gain the all-important purchase on reality. Awareness begins when he asks the question "Where is time leading?" and is activated on his quest. No longer passively awash (like Mountolive) in the inexorable, he searches for the "order and coherence" to patterns, realizing that until he circumscribes things within the orbit of his own powers and sensibilities—until, to put it bluntly, he becomes "god"— and breaks from the orbit of chaos and flux, he cannot be a writer.

In a small but archetypal way Darley does battle with time. Time is the enemy that may pull against him or pull him back; it is also, he learns from Clea, the ally that propels him forward by the "momentum of those feelings . . . of which we ourselves are least conscious." For all intents and purposes Darley masters history, does not become a slave to it, does not become bricked up by it. And the unleashing of his unconsciousness in all its ambivalence—worked out in no particular way, but seen through the gradual rejection of sexual excess and the maturing in love—allows lucid participation in the extent of memory. Once, that is, he deserts chronology, he is able to let loose memory's floodgates.

> Between sleep and waking I lay, feeling the tug of memory's heavy plumb-line: tug of the leaf-veined city which my memory had peopled with masks, malign and beautiful at once. I should see Alexandria again, I knew, in the elusive temporal fashion of a ghost—for once you become aware of the operation of a time which is not calendar-time you become in some sort a ghost.[10]

As Darley grows aware that memory must be manipulated, he can reconstruct the past more accurately. Nor is he any longer a slave to memory. Moving as a ghost out of the dimensionlike holds of time and space, he likewise is able to incorporate time. Time becomes physical and personal at last, even to this ghost operating in the dimensionless world of the past. Like Proust's *moments bienheureux* or Joyce's "epiphanies," Darley's compression of past, present, and future is felt through "bayonets of time." Time comes in by way of these shock waves, the visceral probings to which the artist responds and for which in every way he is responsible.

The tough-minded extension of this unique image is linked with the "wound and the bow" theory—the theory that the artist creates out of his own blood, the act of creation being equally one of destruction. And in essence it is through Darley that Alexandria is destroyed. Such metaphorical bayonets become literal lances of creation and destruction: the harpoon by which Clea is pinned to the sunken ship, and the knife by which Darley (her lover, whose whole life has been an open wound of love) cuts off her hand—a double, necessary act of mutilation. More than grandstand or grand guignol, the scene reverses the clichéd sea-time image formulated by Darley in *Justine*. Indeed, one might read it as an allegorical reversal—the artist snatched from time, triumphing over it, and going on (as Clea and Darley do) to triumph through art.

One need not allegorize however. While the submergence of the artist in these primal and primitive forces—sex, love, birth, death—can be seen as mythopoeic, or even archetypal, Darley's representative emergence into artistic and historic freedom (the past, once delivered, is now only fit for fiction) is no less than the straightforward initiation of writer and man. Freedom is fathered by art—one of the reasons that various protagonists (in the *Quartet* and elsewhere in the other sequences) who happen not to be artists sense how strongly, though not strangely, deterministic life is.

Moving in space freed from time must always appear to the critical and analytical intelligence more exciting than moving in time without space. For the artist, art cannot but appear more intimate and meaningful than life itself, even when art supposedly *is* life itself. For Darley, the artist who comes of age in the *Quartet*, and for Durrell, who implies that this is the way such genesis comes about, the supreme artistic vision is that fine re-creation and balancing of all three things comprising time—history, imagination, memory; the supreme artist is one who can turn the common stuff of realities into triumphs of art; and the supreme art is that which all the while seeks to gain the "purchase on reality," to become ever stable while it is ever changing.

4

Anthony Burgess
The *Malayan Trilogy*: The Futility of History

Future historians will need no tomes to chart the choke, sob, and death rattle of the British Empire in the twentieth century. A few verses of Kipling, one or two pieces by Conrad, Waugh, and Forster, an essay by Orwell indicate the intellectual and ideological rift between pukka sahib and native, and lead us into those pockets of cultural confusion that have become the cul-de-sacs of imperialism. To read—if not to believe—Spengler or Toynbee is to know that whether empire wends its way eastward or westward, going in one direction long enough must bring it back to the beginning. A flourishing culture is incipiently a perishing one, the cycle of history being ineluctable, the seeds of imperialism begetting the roots of its own destruction.

About this, English writers have generally proved sanguine Cassandras, loath to view the setting of Britain's sun apocalyptically. Instead they write nostalgically, ironically, dispassionately (or only intermittently passionately) of the end of colonialism, because, one imagines, the empire has been going out with a whimper and not a bang, and because the real holocausts and catastrophes of our century have outweighed the relatively minor frustrations accruing from British absentee landlordism.

Still, these accounts are monuments to the decline and

fall of a once-great power. If they have anything like a major theme in common it is the social, political, and mental attrition of the ruler, who, through iron-fisted tactics or humanitarian impulses that have proved equally effete, must at last buckle to the gigantic, hard, irresistible will of the ruled. In the colonial realms of diminishing returns, attrition is no more geopolitical phenomenon; it is a psychological and spiritual one, as the author of "Shooting an Elephant," the Kurtz of *Heart of Darkness*, the Mrs. Moore of *A Passage to India* discover. Attrition has been naturally easier to understand post facto than in its stages. And what gradually erodes the foundations of empire, what gradually contributes to its decay, has proved the more complex and valuable confrontation between the writer and his subject.

One of the most contemporary pictures of Britain's nagging *Götterdammerung* is the Malayan trilogy of Anthony Burgess, called in the American edition *The Long Day Wanes*. In theme and action these three novels—running together to a little over five hundred pages—set about to show the twilight of British rule in Malaya and the dawn of freedom for the Malayan states. Burgess's fidelity in treating the problems of a nation that has often seemed about as fathomable as a gibber of apes at a conference table opens new doors of perception on unpublicized reaches of empire and on the failed British mission. Less interested in exploring the hypersensitivity of Forster's "good" Indians and "bad" Englishmen (or vice versa), the metaphysics of evil of Conrad's, or the grotesque parodies of institutions and people of Waugh's darker continents, Burgess, a writer of wit and incredible verbal control, digs in to the nitty-gritty of the political, religious, and cultural mess in the Far East.

What he comes up with is a tragi-comic view of imperialism and an anatomy of the heart of Malaya. In technique Burgess is close to Waugh, but in sensibility he is closer to Orwell. Both understand the tempers of peoples pitted against the Western brand of progress, self-consciously and nationalistically dedicated to their emergence. But unlike Orwell, who views Burma as a force of homogeneous wills (and consequently *one* will) bent upon undermining and overturning the white man's power, Burgess sees Malaya in all its heterogeneity; sees its timeless conflicts arising as much from indigenous human nature as from abstractions like "brutality and jingoism" (to quote Orwell on Kipling) of imperialism; sees its people given to the same vices, vanities, frustrations, desires, and excesses, be they black, white, or yellow, English, Chinese, Eurasian, Malaysian, or Indian, Christian, Moslem, Buddhist, or Hindu.

Tough-minded, at bottom an ironist and comedian rather than a satirist, Burgess keeps the proper artistic distance from problems that obviously speak for themselves. Yet he is anything but cautious and tentative. The opening line of the trilogy—"East? They wouldn't know the bloody East if they saw it"—is a headlong plunge into Burgess's central theme: distrust, both intellectually and humanistically, of the historic process, a process made more futile than risky owing to pretense, turpitude, and, most often, simple ignorance. Soft-pedaling the philosophic or emotional implications, Burgess sets out to prove that only empirically must the setting of one sun necessarily mean the rising of another; to prove (as Robert Penn Warren has written of *Nostromo*) that the "moral regeneration of society depends not upon shifts in mechanisms, but upon the moral regeneration of men." [1]

History is chapter and verse of the trilogy, and Victor Crabbe, quondam teacher of history its hero. Crabbe, liberal, sensual, dry, superior in intellect, conscience, and guilt, displays a comically bungling dexterity in the sure-footed descent that marks his own literal death and the symbolic death of the British Empire in Malaysia. Somehow boosted higher and higher up the tottering ladder of administrative school posts, but nevertheless grown more ineffectual in his ability to strike a rapport all around, Crabbe suffers corresponding personal defeats, deteriorating in his physical and social habits, withdrawing into a shell of cynicism, scuttling randomly—as befits his name —over the flotsam and jetsam of his life, a life of failures without successes, nadirs without climaxes, battles without victor-ease. Crabbe's move from disillusionment and disaffection to alienation, from dissipation to revulsion, from sordidness and impotence to an absurd death, counterpoints the rise of Malaysia and contrasts ironically the sudden agony of individual change with the impersonal, maddeningly leisurely forward march of events.

Throughout the trilogy, history and hero interpenetrate. Both are extremely viable, history being for Burgess not memory but the living pattern that Crabbe (agent, reflector, commentator, pawn) experiences. By living in the present, Crabbe hopes to escape, or at least blot out a past that he dreads. ("Memory had no significance . . . dreams were not memory," he muses before his shaving mirror. The gulf between *The Long Day Wanes* and *The Music of Time*, or the *Alexandria Quartet*, or, to a lesser degree, *Strangers and Brothers* is, over so singular a theme as memory and the past, immense.) Crabbe's psyche, however, is but part of Burgess's historic perspective and his novelistic method. Underplaying the sense of the past which in the timeless East doesn't exist anyway, or at most exists uniformly—"Malaya . . . warm, slummy comfort as permanent as the surrounding mountain-jungle"—and focusing on what is immediate and palpable, Burgess paints continuous pictures of English and Malaysian "history," and impels into the cycle the dead past, the fluctuating present, the unpredictable, but certain, future.

Via James Joyce—Burgess is a Joycean scholar as well as a practicing disciple—has come, undoubtedly, a concern with Vico and cyclical theories of history. Burgess is less attracted by Vico's general laws of growth, decay, and regrowth through which all civilizations must pass, than by his analogy of civilizations evolving parallel to children developing—acquiring knowledge, that is, through growing experience. Thus with Crabbe and thus with Malaya. As freedom dawns for the new nation, in the jungle is written the ironic coda to his own education. Journeying upriver to investigate the murder of a colonial—a journey that invites comparison with Marlowe's in *Heart of Darkness* and Tony Last's in *A Handful of Dust*—Crabbe meets the rubber-planter George Costard, symbol of British Toryism and the foundering empire.

> I'm in this game to keep something alive that's very, very beautiful. The feudal tradition, the enlightened patriarchal principle. You people have been throwing it all away, educating them to revolt against us. They won't be happy, any of them. It's only on the estates now that the old ideas can be preserved. I'm the father of these people. They can look up to me, bring me their troubles and let me participate in their joys. Don't you think that's good and beautiful? They're my children, all of them. I correct them, I cherish them, I show them the way they should go.[2]

In this slightly irregular Viconian mirror, Crabbe sees reflected the distorted shapes of his own education. The past, now almost totally suppressed, rises before him when he inadvertently discovers that Costard was the lover of his first wife, now dead, drowned when a car Crabbe was driving skidded on an English country road and plunged into an icy river. Illuminated, disillusioned, limping from a scorpion bite—one of Burgess's many "touches"—Crabbe slips as he is boarding the temporarily deserted launch that took him up river and himself drowns.

Hegelian thought, too, sifts through *The Long Day Wanes*. The interpreter of Vico for the post-Renaissance world, the intellectual antecedent of Spengler and Toynbee, Hegel placed the keystone, if not the foundation, of the arch through which all modern students of history must pass. Cold, precise, deterministic in its metaphysics, the Hegelian dialectic is both logical and phenomenological, but ultimately antihumanistic and ethically deplorable to anyone who sees the historical process continually renewing itself at the expense of human beings, to anyone who views as hopeless and nihilistic a process by which ends not only justify means, but are sacrificed to them. Thesis, antithesis, synthesis; the unholy trinity of materialism! And the synthesis that becomes a new thesis in this eternal genesis of organization and reorganization may be stronger, though not necessarily better, as Burgess suggests at the opening of the trilogy's final volume, *Beds in the East*.

> Dawn of freedom for yet another nation, freedom and all the rest of the abstractions. Dawn, dawn, dawn, and people waking up with various kinds of mouths and carried-forwards of the night or day before. Dawn, anyway.[3]

One other appendage of the Hegelian doctrine is sportively twisted by Burgess: the belief that great men are those whose personal aims coincide with the aims of history. For Burgess, there are no such men; or, with Joyce's Bloom or Earwicker, one man becomes "allmen," great and small. Crabbe runs the gamut of historic personages, metamorphosed in thought into Hamlet, Aeneas, Theseus, Don Quixote, Ulysses(the title of the trilogy is a line from the Tennyson poem), and Caesar. The coda to the sequence—a liberation-day party at which Crabbe's secretary is seen crying in her crab mousse—is, in fact, a memento mori on his historical effectiveness. "Poor Victor . . . poor, poor Victor," she sobs. "He came, he saw, he conquered," responds a young subaltern. "Victor ludorum." [4] Victor of the games! The allusion and bilingual pun ironically formulate Crabbe: a tragi-comic Caesar, failed in apparently the simplest of missions, the least meaningful of intrigues, the most rudimentary of relationships.

Antihero Victor Crabbe (Victoria Cross for inconspicuous bravery?) is also an anti-Hegelian who has lost his cool as well as his dialectic. He is, though part of the historical flux, at odds with it, undermined by his romanticism and hopelessly clashing with the impenetrable will, the immovable spirit, the inscrutable mind of the East. Like yet another Joycean hero—the Stephen Dedalus of *Ulysses*—Crabbe teaches history, and he, too, is trying to awake from its nightmarish provisos—not the "cry in the streets" of "dear, dirty, Dublin," but the slow-motion antics of Malaysian life that too easily draw one into forgetfulness. Images of sleep, beds, drunkenness sift through the trilogy, beginning with the titles of individual books. The first, *Time for a Tiger*, alludes to the brand name of a potent, stupefying beer; the second, *The Enemy in the Blanket*, to potential surrender to expatriation and Eastern sensuousness; the last, *Beds in the East*—a quotation from *Antony and Cleopatra*—to relaxation of all responsibility and, ironically, loveless total abandonment.

These irresistible forces must finally get the better of Crabbe. We first meet him fitfully sleeping next to his wife, Fenella; and, morning after morning, he wakes to neglect her, to seek out sordid liaisons, to twit his su-

periors, to alienate his colleagues and friends, to fall prey
to enemies—potentially every native is the white man's
enemy—lurking in the blanket. Even for Westerners
"the patterns of the East are few." But Crabbe's life of
plod and monotony reflects less an actual resistance to
change than a flouting of Establishment codes. It is
ideologism, not apathy, nor egoism, nor even idealism
that carries him over the ruts. His vulnerability, erosion,
death are forged by the desire to dissipate a particular
vision of human life and culture cherished for hundreds
of years by the anomaly known as British colonial: one
who through an infectious romanticism has preserved
enchantment (albeit superficial) with the dreamy poetry
and retard of the East, and (worse) a patronizing charity
toward its natives.

> The romantic dream . . . was no longer appropriate
> to an age in which sleep was impossible. The whole
> East was awake, building dams and canals, power-
> houses and car factories, forming committees, drawing
> up constitutions, having selected from the West the
> few tricks it could understand and use. . . . Liberal-
> ism, itself a romantic dream had long gone under . . .
> and there was no longer any room for the individual,
> there was nothing now that any one man could
> build. . . . It was time he cleared the romantic jungle
> in which he wanted to lurk, acknowledged that life
> was striving not dreaming, and planted the seeds of a
> viable relationship.[5]

Thus autistically, and by soft lies, we bridge the way
things were and the way things are, and, like Crabbe,
become the dupe of our best intentions and failed reso-
lutions. The intention to shrug off this somnolence so
sanely and keenly inveighed against is perfectly count-
ered by the desire not to. "Good, too, Logic, of course;
in itself, but not in fine weather" runs an epigraph to

the sequence. Ambivalence, not speciousness, gnaws at Crabbe. Inching forward with Malaysia and loosing it for independence, or retreating and devouring the lotus of indolence; these are choices that neither entirely exclude nor entirely complement each other. Malaysia, the East are of themselves ambivalent. On the surface, the daily comedy of quarrels, flurries, peccadilloes, laissez faire, innocent trespasses on ingrained but passé taboos; below, the whirring, demonic dynamo. The East, as Burgess sees it, is both active and passive, containing the principles of yin and yang, humming at both poles of the dialectic at once: a phenomenon alien to the West, which, nurtured on Hegelian propositions, submits to the certainty of either cyclical or linear progression.

Change and no change, history and no history are the paradoxes Crabbe wrestles with and cannot master, just as the East itself is seemingly unable to master its master paradox, everywhere displayed but nowhere decipherable: starved and naked Communist guerrillas in the jungle, luxury and decadence in the cities; the deadly logic of revolution confronting the politics of conservatism; gracious, civil protocol facing "ambushers, eviscerations, beheadings"; the thrust for freedom vis-à-vis complacency; primitive magic against rationalism, polygamy against prostitution, life cult against death cult.

It is not difficult to understand Crabbe's obsession with history throughout *The Long Day Wanes*. History-less forces, built up over thousands of years, are suddenly pushing him onto the threshold of discovery, and, as inert as he is, impelling him over the detritus of the lives of the Westerners who have escaped from timelessness into the mainstream of history: Nabby Adams, Fenella Crabbe, Rupert Hardman. All, despite their weaknesses, were fighting the lure of the East, refusing to remain cloddish or to become, in the final sense, absorbed.

"Absorbed" is a motif that begins metaphorically and

ends in earnest literalness. The word evokes and controls contexts of thought, as much Burgess's as Crabbe's. Little ambiguity remains after the extended interplay of definitions. In every sense Crabbe *is* absorbed into the East, into the "head-reeling collocation of cultures," into the emotion, if not the actual rationale of history. The East abstracts, engrosses, engulfs him, only as the pulsation of a timeless body existing as a timeless pattern could.

His colleague, Raj, lightly prophesies early in the trilogy, "The country will absorb you and you will cease to be Victor Crabbe. . . . You will lose function and identity . . . You will be swallowed up." [6] This trifling badinage of the smoking room later becomes a kind of intuitive warning. Crabbe's immediate, sensuous impressions of changeless Kenching (fictitious capital of the fictitious state, Dahaga) surrender to the disturbing realization that the "future would be like the past," that those British who remain in Malaya might also, like the dozens of migrants and conquerors before them, be absorbed. And shortly before his separation from Fenella (more sinned against than sinning), Crabbe takes refuge in the comfort of a cliché, both defensible and admissible, yet nevertheless implying acquiescence to the overwhelming principle. It is the cracking of his carapace, the point of no return. "We've got to be absorbed into these customs. We're still too tough to be ingested quickly, but we've got to try and soften ourselves to a bolus, we've got to yield." [7] Raj's earlier words, flashing through Crabbe's mind during the fatal journey into the interior, now become converted into an ironic anti-prophecy as he rejects the idea of "his never going home, his complete assimilation to the country . . . [his] leaving his bones up river . . . the grave quickly becoming a native shrine to be loaded with supplicatory bananas and flowers." [8] What indeed happens so absurdly to

Scobie in the *Alexandria Quartet* happens grotesquely to Crabbe. History is past master at distorting, at giving the lie. "History [Crabbe comments vehemently on the launch] . . . the best thing is to put all that in the books and forget about it. . . . We've got to throw up the past otherwise we can't live in the present. The past has got to be killed." [9] Crabbe, of course, who is the past for the East *is* killed, while the Indian veterinarian Vythilingham, professionally and ideologically removed from that great abstraction "humanity" for which Crabbe so ungainly sacrifices himself, looks dispassionately on. Crabbe struggles and subsides, his body absorbed into the river, his spirit into "jungle, river and sky," his class and empire into a Malaysia that foreshadows an absorption, as ironic as his own, into the past and history.

Like Tony Last's or Jay Gatsby's death, Victor Crabbe's symbolizes the dissipation of an illusion, the end of an era, and consequently is charged socially and morally. But his remains a psychological disaster. For Burgess is at hard core a realist who believes in character and in creating believable characters. Crabbe's psychological rout is predictable, though nonetheless eloquent. Once he begins growing in awareness—and it isn't long into the novel before he does—perceptions multiply so rapidly that he barely has time to take stock of them; their diversity and intensity, as well as his own sensitivity, undermine him. Burgess calls Crabbe into life not only amidst a confusion of cultures but amidst a profusion of "things." We know Crabbe as much from his sensations as from his revelations; not least of all the attraction for, the total immersion in, the sensuousness and movement of a Malaysia teeming with "mosques and . . . muezzins," fishmongers and magic, "shadow-plays about mythical heroes, bull-fights and cock-fights . . . axeing, love-potions, coconuts, rice, the eternal rule of the Abang." [10]

We know Crabbe, too, from the other characters who, at times, so dominate that he becomes a weaker, partially a subordinate, figure. The technique, an old one, is in the great tradition of the English comic novel, which, from Fielding on, has basically been the novel of memorable minor types. It is this peripheral world of *The Long Day Wanes* that is in many ways more remarkable and less remote than the central one of Crabbe's consciousness. It is the periphery of Durrell's Alexandria, of Powell's London, of Mrs. Manning's Bucharest and Athens; a periphery that evokes the fullness of Darley or Jenkins or Guy and Harriet Pringle; that energizes the sequence and prevents its falling (as too often the case with Snow or Mrs. Lessing) into unrelieved intellectual patterns.

These sometimes tragic, generally comic, foils to Crabbe are individually set in each section. Nabby ("Abel") Adams, the beer-swilling sergeant of police, boondoggler par excellence and perhaps Burgess's best single creation in the trilogy, hulks through *Time for a Tiger* with Rabelaisian appetite and lustiness—a warm, natural, giant of a man, exaggerating through expansiveness and instinct Crabbe's constriction and inertia. Adams is a kind of idle Hercules, nonintellectually absorbing the East, while Crabbe, the misguided, beset Atlas, labors under it, shouldering its burdens, crushed by it in the end.

And so, almost, is Rupert Hardman, lawyer, who occupies most of the second book. Hardman, a practicing expatriate riddled with *Weltschmerz*, seeks to revitalize himself, mend his finances, and "become" the East through his marriage to Che Normah—a sort of "bathycolpic" Wife of Bath—which entails surrender of identity through change of name and conversion to the Moslem faith. Hardman is a step beyond Nabby and one before Crabbe, for he wishes, at first, to play no role, to match—at its simplest level—the thing for the fact.

But if Nabby can absorb, and Crabbe be absorbed, Hardman can do neither. Nor can he convince himself that a cycle of Cathay is better than fifty years of Europe, and so defects for England, deserting his pregnant, though still inordinately nympholeptic wife on a voyage to the Holy Land.

In part three are the separate stories of Rosemary Michael and Robert Loo. Rosemary, "black but comely," evoking delights of "houris, harems, and beds scented with Biblical spices," is a naïve, pliant sex-pot, obsessed with the idea of marrying a European, and through most of the novel hoping that Joe, current in her formidable list of white lovers ("she could not stand the touch of brown fingers"), will call her to England and to the finest society. Robert is a musically precocious and sexually repressed young Chinese, who, in his father's restaurant, amidst the babble of voices and blare of the jukebox, against the "cyclorama of tins of mild and corned beef," composes symphonies. Rosemary and Robert, one in comic pretentiousness, the other in pathetic earnest, are also heirs of two cultures. Both are in the rudimentary stages of sophistication; without having fully abdicated their birthright as children of the East, they display, unwittingly, the inverse yearning of East for West. Both, too, in their frustrations and desires, express the birth pangs and confusion of the coming Malaysia; and both are "pursued" by the West: she by a farcically lecherous stage Turk ("a Muslim . . . who looked like a European"); he, in quite another way, by Crabbe, who dreams of his (Loo's) becoming free Malaysia's first serious composer.

Nabby Adams, Rupert Hardman, Rosemary Michael, and Robert Loo represent two faces, East and West, and are set apart from Crabbe; or rather, being of another breed, he is excluded from their ken. He functions differently. Though they are introspective, though they live under the zodiac of individualized obsessions—snobbery of caste, religion, position or race, desire for power, wealth, women or motor cars, dedication to drinking, lusting, or fornicating—their *idée fixe* is not, like Crabbe's, universal. Like most who rarely intellectualize the condition of life, they accept it or do not accept it; but at all events know what they want. As extraordinary and eccentric as Burgess's characters may be, their concern is with realities, not abstractions. Burgess, in his comic wisdom, has seen how we are all tragically self-centered. Even while a nation vibrates with new consciousness and hope as it stands ready to leap into freedom, its people are concerned with their petty, immediate, (to them) significant lives, with, in short, palpable truth, not any sort of enduring one. They opt for "human lives . . . not humanity." Crabbe easily becomes the outsider. Hagridden by ideals and the idea of humanity with which he can inspire no one, he drives against self-interest and the ethos—randomly, moodily, finally morbidly questing after an impossible dream.

Thus, while others seem to shift or balance, Crabbe is the only one who properly changes, moving as he does vertically as well as horizontally. The drama within is played all the while against the externalities—against those who remain or depart, against Malaysia, against class and country—and against the crucial constant, time itself, by which, through which, he is supported and undermined. Time marks his psychical and cyclical risings and fallings, time marks the incurrent awareness that his powers are waning along with the long day, and time seemingly marks, its own inherent paradox: the Western concept of time, that is, being at odds with and useless in an East where time is beyond conventional construction. Crabbe's change often seems violent, as any change would seem violent in a world where time is standing still; and the process of change here, too, is an inverted one, marked by the regularity of a negative time.

This is much less a paradox than it appears, though the effect is curious. Through a rain of Eastern languages (snatches of seven, all told), through precise, idiomatic dialogue, and through a rhetoric that can do somersaults, in places even shoot off rockets, Burgess captures the flowing immediacy of the present. Yet running side by side, from beginning to end, is a feeling countering the present, a feeling of opaqueness and sameness. There are scenes of soliloquy and stream-of-consciousness—the most controlled techniques for rendering time slowly—and the iteration of motifs (especially words like "time-lessness," "changelessness," "unchanging") that have a dying fall, impinging upon our senses as much as upon Crabbe's, and slowing down action to a standstill.

Metaphorically Crabbe is lured by the life around him into the endless sea of time. Yet being an occidental he fights against its breakers. Not so the oriental, who knows that time is timeless, that inaction is the way of the East and the great Lao-tse, and that, logically, inaction is therefore timeless. It's useless to understand, pinpoint, analyze it with such extrusive philosophies that Europeans like Vico, Hegel, Bergson, or Einstein propound. Asia contemplates time, does not resist it, bathes, and becomes awash in it. This is the hardest lesson for Crabbe, and he learns it only by giving up trying to understand it and abdicating all occidental sensibilities, but learns it much too late.

Time, impinging in the East with the force of time-lessness, charts Crabbe's change, not rigorously but through loose stages, outlined objectively as well as sub-jectively. Burgess's point in using the omniscient narrator is to sift the psyche of the East almost simultaneously with that of Crabbe, imparting a realistic or naturalistic flavor to the novel, and keeping it always on the pitch of discovery in true *Bildungsroman* fashion.

Perspectives shift in time—it is yet another of the ways

in which we watch Crabbe change—but time itself, the immovable blackcloth, scarcely shifts at all. The idea, simple as it is cosmic, logical as it is persistent, burgeons out of the East, rooted as much in providence as in passivity or "mere impossibility." A word, a concept, a way of life controls the idea. It is *Tida' apa.*

> "*Tida' apa*" meant so much more than "It doesn't matter" or "Who cares?" There was something indefinable and satisfying about it, implying that the universe would carry on, the sun shine, the durians fall.[11]

To the mind of the East *Tida' apa* is psychologically and temporally the reflex action of inaction, implying that all change, being the same, is therefore useless and unnecessary; an oriental *Weltanschauung* that even today—the trilogy dates from 1956—has not completely been dissipated, despite Japan's leap from isolation to world conquest, despite the dramatic rise of communism in China, Korea, Vietnam, or Malaysia itself. For many, *Tida' apa* —apart from its stoic or quasi-religious connotations— bespeaks a certain optimism for the East, whereas for the West inevitability or fatality is viewed pessimistically. And to the Western mind, decadent in its glut of progress, *Tida' apa* seems sheer nihilism, somewhat more frightening, in fact, for being nihilistic and positive together.

The phrase causes at first mild rebellion in Crabbe, intent on shoring up the ruins of his own past by building anew a future for the Malaysians.

> The process of which . . . he was a part was an ineluctable process. His being here, in a brown country, sweltering in an alien classroom, was prefigured and ordained by history. For the end of the Western pattern was the conquest of time and space. But out of time and space came point-instants, and out of point-

instants came a universe. So it was right that he stood here now, teaching the East about the Industrial revolution, [about how to] judge Shakespeare by the Aristotelian yardstick, hear five-part counterpoint and find it intelligible.[12]

But it is not right, neither for them nor for Crabbe. Here can be seen the first moment of a dissolving dialectic, as Crabbe rationalizes from inevitability, justifies the wrenching of segments from history to fit the case. It is, like his indiscretions of the ego and libido, born of an infatuation for what is novel in the Orient. Crabbe courts the Orient as a lover, still hidebound by his wife, courts a mistress. His real wife, Fenella, comes to fully realize what his laxity prevents him from ever realizing, that Western values cannot easily be subsumed in novelty for very long, that there must always be atavistic clashes between East and West. Fenella, a hypersensitive woman, and a painstaking, if not terribly good poet, writes a poem about Malaysia, describing it as a land where time has no movement, where the hours "set like ice-cubes," where people live "in sight of that constant eye" of the sun, where the "beasts" live in "day's denomination." Fenella sees how impossible it is for the Westerner to live in the timeless, monolithic present that blots out or buries the past: to scrap, that is, the time and space continuum of history for the "point–instants" of the universe of *Tida' apa*.

Fenella's poem does momentarily spur Crabbe's longing for England. It comes at a pivotal point in the novel, a point about which he can spin back and recover some of his past, a point after which he cannot. Crabbe remains committed, fearing that relaxation of hope will cut him off even further from human intercourse; fearing, too, the botch he knows the Malaysians will make of their first months of independence without some steady hand, a fear both truistically and altruistically founded.

The assistant headmaster, Jaganathan, an ugly, pompous, jealous sort, hopeful of taking over upon independence, unwittingly helps sever further Crabbe's ties with the West. Blackmailing Crabbe about his various revolutionary activities and writings as an undergraduate in England with the intention of bullying and bending him, has precisely the opposite effect. For while Jaganathan's naïveté and buffoonery in matters of Establishment college-Communists (though the paranoia over communism in Malaysia is still neither simple nor comic), infuriates Crabbe, it also churns up a stony nostalgia for an idealism spawned in the now-dead world of his salad days. It confirms his ties with the East, revives him, alerts him once again to the viability of continuance and change.

Crabbe really feels that he can be instrumental in building the new Malaysia. As the novel moves toward its denouement and peripeteia, Crabbe, the raw ideals of youth transformed at last into middle-aged thoughts of purpose, moves toward the timeless dream of history. Despite general antagonisms, despite many troublesome persons like Jaganathan, despite anxiety over irrevocable choices, despite having cut himself off from his wife, despite all self-castigations, he regains, with something of the earlier intensity, this vitalizing idealism.

> Crabbe looked at himself [in the mirror]: hair now riding back from his forehead, the beginning of a jowl. He looked down at his paunch, pulled it in, flinched at the effort, let it out again. He thought it was perhaps better to be middle-aged, less trouble. That growing old was a matter of volition was a discovery he had only recently made, and it pleased him. It was infantile, of course, like the pleasure of controlling excretion, but transitional periods in history had always appealed to him most—Silver Ages, Hamlet

phases, when past and future were equally palpable, and opposing, could produce current.[13]

This is not the voice of a Prufrock—though in a kind of Eliotesque extension Crabbe does find the "objective correlative" for his own middle-aged transition in the transition of Malaysia—but of a Leopold Bloom. Life, and it is significant that it *is* life, is affirmed, placed (however ironically things may turn out) in the framework of renewed discovery. Nor is it Crabbe's fault entirely that such affirmation casts a long, fatal, negative shadow. Given the fickle premises of history and the argument of change, the conclusion is inevitable. For Malaysia, the past must become one thing; for Crabbe, another—the bridge to his death. This all-important bridge—somewhat shakily constructed at the eleventh hour by Burgess, considering the weight it must carry—leads from logic to metaphysics. With the recognition that the past, England, "the mandarin world" is dead—a recognition reached by travels over the rough roads of Fenella's melancholia, Hardman's eloquence, Costard's slightly hysterical jeremiads—Crabbe immerses himself in the timeless dream most completely. This is Burgess's *coup de théâtre* in *The Long Day Wanes*. Crabbe drowns.

But the *Malayan Trilogy* is not just a composite of rhetorical fripperies, wit, puns, flirtations with language, and love affairs with technique. It is not merely a comedy of misplaced idealism, alienation, despair, impotence, or transparent ideologies—though it is, of course, all these as well. It is foremost a continuing drama of change: how one man encounters and experiences it, founders upon and succumbs to it. It is a novel of one man borne by one current while beating against another, of one hard-shelled but vulnerable, of one aloof but involved, of one not deep, but sensitive and sincere. It is a novel of one better than so many, yet, in the end, not quite sufficient.

Though Crabbe does battle with the snobbism and mediocrity of his own class and with the indolence and insouciance of Malaysia, he is, when all is tallied, perhaps a crusty vestige of that Western liberalism and humanitarianism that has historically proved so ineffectual. As the "timeless dream"—a motif not only insistent but impossible to escape—history is futile. Yet one goes on in spite of it, does not surrender because of it. For the sense of the present for the East is ever omnipresent, blotting out the past, ordaining the future. Crabbe's own early musings on the finality of the past, the fiction of history ("a kind of story" is how he defines it for his class) anticipates the conclusion to the novel as well as provides precise commentary on history's futility:

> It was unnatural to give life to the dead [i.e., through memory]. The dead are fractured, atomized, dust in the sunlight, dregs in the beer. Yet the fact of love remains and to love the dead is, in the nature of things, impossible. One must love the living, the living fractured and atomized into individual bodies and minds that can never be close, never be important. For if one were to mean more than the others, then we should be back again, identifying and, with sudden shocks, contrasting, and bringing the dead back to life. The dead are dead.[14]

Throughout the trilogy, Crabbe, for all his major failings, abides by this philosophy, is filled with this sort of love. He is all too human—one who, like most, revels in great victories but most often welters in little failures. He worships the living and the promise of living, but for him, as for England, the day has waned. The present, which was once the future for the past, will now become the past for the future. And Crabbe, a victor-come-lately, like the very stork of the night who comes last (as a second epigraph to the novel has it) and is "torn to pieces" while the others "get them gone," has been sacrificed to this irresistible historic principle, symbolized so often in the sequence by the eternal sun—the image of timelessness itself—that has set before, will set again, on countless, weary empires.

5

C. P. Snow
Strangers and Brothers: The Morality of History

C. P. Snow, the dynamic, prolific apostle to the two
cultures, scientific and humanistic, has made some stunning contributions to the thought of the postwar years.
By immersing himself in virtually every eventful intellectual flood of the past decade—science, literature, business, education, government—and by having swum to
the top, Snow, through a high-caliber dilettantism that
can only be envied, has proved himself a distinctive, if
not wholly influential voice, and of enormous, if not original, resources. Snow's legacy, and his most sustained attempt at codifying fictionally the dilemmas and direc-
tions of our age, is the long novel sequence, *Strangers
and Brothers,* begun in 1940 and only recently completed.
The eleven volumes are the works of a clear, intelligent,
logical, and synthesizing mind, one rigorously devoted to
the human condition, on that grasps the realpolitik of society's functioning (or, in many cases, malfunctioning)
on every conceivable level.

Qualities like these should foster compelling and exciting fiction, but such, alas, is not the case. For all their
concern with man's fate and with society's burning issues,
Snow's themes seem in too many ways procrustean beds
for his ill-fitting characters; and his settings, for all their
societal crosscutting, are in the end battlegrounds on
which armies of logic (with Snow as field-marshal) do

battle over personal morality and public expedience. It is too easy to conclude (as F. R. Leavis and Malcolm Muggeridge each has in his notorious way) that Snow is arrogant and inflated, an unquestionably articulate but sorrowfully incomplete talent, swelling with apologies for the Establishment, bolstering mediocrity, and foisting his fiats on the world at large. For conversely, Snow is equally one of the sole remaining advocates of reason and compromise in an hysterically intractable world growing progressively more insane. Yet in all truth this ameliorating myopia of Snow's cannot be divorced from the aesthetic deficiencies of his fiction. In the last and crucial analysis he lacks the all-around poetic vision that enables him to see man as other than a social being, that admits man's physical and metaphysical needs, and, most regretfully, lacks a novelistic intuition that allows man to grow out of a communal history and into a life of his own.

All this reduces to the one thing that may be the alpha and omega of Snow's work in the novel: each character is seen as an exponent of a rational, efficient, and often higher morality but rarely, as our lifetime and philosophies have repeatedly confirmed, a comic or tragic thing in himself. In his mission as regulator of the two cultures, Snow has gone so far as to tell us that science (which he takes as a robust handmaiden to civilization) is gradually enriching our lives by expanding the potentialities of our will and, consequently, by limiting the areas of tragedy. Science can innoculate us against the temptation to poke about in our souls, can make us immune to "defeat, self-indulgence, and moral vanity." [1] Snow realizes that art has seldom been born of healthy parents, that sickness has in fact generated it; but in his utilitarianism he chooses the road to health over the road to art—at the expense of his writing. His fiction of morality—impeded more than aided by the naturalistic technique and unframed by either comedy or tragedy (which may coalesce as they do in Powell or Durrell)—becomes too often pallid, boring, and lifeless.

Unavoidably Snow must look at things—even fiction —from the point of view of the scientist. Unlike Zola's naturalism, which overlays science on artistic realism or impressionism, Snow's emerges from scientific precepts that are only then decked out with trappings of plot, character, and theme. A Snow novel becomes in every sense a problem and a syllogism. Thematically any one of them could be entitled "the affair"; technically each is an experiment. Logical men posit logical theories about logical happenings, and, given free play, free will, and the proper laboratory conditions, posit logical conclusions dictated by logical proofs.

It is small wonder that Snow couches pronouncements on fiction in the metaphors and jargon closer to science (*pace* I. A. Richards) than literary criticism. Distinguishing between great novels and merely good ones, he has found the latter overburdened with a "continuum of feeling" and lacking in "causal psychological insight." [2] (Incidentally Snow makes good sense on these points.) And his own procedure in *Strangers and Brothers*, he tells us, is the "use of a thematic system to organize a fair mass of material." [3]

Snow's impartial partiality for the scientific method has proved unfortunate for his fiction, but not disastrous. His direct, if limited procedure is actually the groundwork for one of the more self-contained approaches to the novel sequence, an extension in "width and depth" of certain central themes. When it comes to organizing and solidifying these themes qua themes, Snow is master. Work of this sort, however, is but one-half a novelist's job; and Snow is hard pressed to make the required division between the aesthetics and technics of his novels. Compared with Powell, say, who is also concerned with extension in width and depth, but who manages it through the shifting interplay of people as they move through time, Snow counterpoints the lives of his characters against a droning ground bass of history, finding that situations do not so much change as recur, and that there is a continuity, not disparity, between past and present events. *Strangers and Brothers* ultimately concerns the viability, justness, and equitableness of time, as it applies to the individual, as it applies to society. Time is the great arbitrator and ameliorator that works things out. Snow's is the morality of history.

The surrogate intelligence that records the historic continuity of events in the series is Lewis Eliot. Seemingly motivated by a thousand passions and conflicts, Eliot moves from obscurity to success; he is cool, flexible, enterprising, yet lacking any real personality. His greatest change has been from an easygoing bore into a crashing one; yet Snow has defined the "inner design" of the sequence as the "resonance between what Eliot sees and what he feels." [4] In theory "resonance" would seem the proper word for a physicist-novelist and for the sequence as a whole. The response between a vibratory system (Eliot) and applied forces (society and its various themes) suggests a vital and continuous exchange of amplification, but it is often difficult to tune in on Eliot's vibrations, detect his impulses, or gauge his soundings. Despite Snow's own gloss on the idea of resonance— "Some of the more important emotional themes [Eliot] observes through others' experience, and then finds them enter into his own"—there is a disparity between materials with merely anecdotal interest and those with novelistic relevance. Snow, in other words, is frequently recalcitrant about refashioning older materials of potential significance into meaningful shapes.

Take for example a scene from *Time of Hope*. Eliot, a poor boy, whose father has just gone bankrupt, contributes ten shillings ("twice as much" as anyone else, says his proud, possessive mother) toward the class munitions fund (it is 1918). Rather than being heartily applauded for his subscription, Eliot is given a sound verbal drubbing by the master, Peck.

> That's quite a lot of money, friend Eliot. . . . I wonder you can afford it. . . . I wonder you don't feel obliged to put it towards your father's debts. . . . Let me give you a piece of advice, my friend. . . . It will be to your advantage in the long run. . . . It isn't the showy things that are most difficult to do, Eliot. It's just plodding away and doing your duty and never getting thanked for it—that's the test for bright lads like you. You just bear my words in mind.[5]

The incident clearly fixes itself in our minds. Peck's priggishness, his frustration, even his limited sadism (sapped of all interest in view of his tendentiousness) seemingly anticipates an important motif in Eliot's life. Embarrassment, the admonition to guilt, the swipe at pride should be traumatic for an eleven-year-old; a crack novelist would return to the scene again and again. Yet there are no further resonances; the incident is never converted as later occasion demands. Snow, while he has almost no trouble in manufacturing scenes pregnant with latent meaning, has great difficulty in delivering such meaning at the crucial time.

An untapped vignette like this would normally glare from the pages of a single-decker novel, and the possibility of its getting lost in a long sequence should almost preclude its insertion. When Charles Stringham is forcibly put to bed by Widmerpool early on in *The Music of Time,* and states with jovial drunkenness that Widmerpool will be the death of him, Powell foreshadows a symbolic (and perhaps literal) fact. One is keyed to it as the series progresses; there are vibrations set moving within and without the event. But though Eliot does a great deal of "plodding away," fulfilling his obligations to God, king, and country, achieving in addition fame, fortune, and the women he loves, the early incident makes little difference to anyone concerned—Eliot least of all. Potentially deep, clear resonances between things seen and felt more often than not die in a muted twang.

Actually, Snow resonates more successfully with personae who, unlike Eliot, are in a sense movable, though even these are held back owing to certain of the author's critical assumptions. Ironically one thing that retards character development throughout *Strangers and Brothers* is Snow's bias for the historical over the psychological mode. Disclaiming the efficacy of the stream-of-conscious ("moment-by-moment") technique ("not so much a technique as an attitude of mind"), finding it has become arid and sterile, Snow opts for a synthesis of nineteenth and twentieth-century theories of writing novels.

> In knowing a human being, one does not restrict oneself to the seconds ["the solitary moments of free association"] in which one hears him speak and watches his face: one thinks about him, corrects one's thoughts, investigates his past and guesses his future, listens to others' opinions, and gradually forms a kind of composite of feeling and observation [as Eliot is supposed to do one imagines] which, though it includes moment-by-moment pictures, is utterly different in kind.[6]

All this is undoubtedly true in conception, but it can be, and often is, tedious in execution. Composites, whatever else they might be, are seldom the real thing. It takes the power of a Dickens, Dostoyevsky, or Mann to imbue them with life, and writers less than titanic have circumvented the problem in various ways. Powell creates character through accretion, Durrell by shifting and dimensionalizing, Mrs. Lessing by internalization. Snow, however, works with bits and snippets, cutting here, pasting there, until he has not composites so much as collages—patchwork characters set against a moral backdrop.

Fortunately he does at times fight free of theory to score considerable success with character. Roy Calvert, a figure incidental to several of the novels, and the protagonist of *The Light and the Dark* is his most successful attempt. Calvert is, by any standard, inspirationally conceived, being at once logical, vital, confessional, melancholic, anguished, what, in fact, Ivan Karamazov might have been had he grown up in the Midlands and read philosophy at Cambridge. Snow finds the perfect objective correlative for so complex a personality in Calvert's researches into the extinct Sogdian language and his translations of Manichaean liturgy. Calvert's alternation between the light of the spirit and the dark of the flesh, between faith and doubt, his flirtation with élitest philosophies (not excluding National Socialism), and his sexual excesses are passionate and fundamental routes of the alienated twentieth-century intellectual. Though not exposed to multiple views—no character in the sequence can be with a monolithic narrator—his emotions are never fully displaced by the cold rationale of Eliot, nor does he ever become a disembodied ideal or moral analogue. Calvert moves horizontally in time as well as vertically in space. He demonstrates an historic justness in his symbolic movement from the political fervor and vacillation of the thirties to the nihilism of the forties, but his progress is psychologically realistic at the same time.

Calvert, as a shy, intelligent, sensitive youth makes his initial appearance in *Strangers and Brothers*. His gift of an expensive cigarette case to Jack Cotery, a clerk on the local newspaper owned by the senior Calvert, is the gratuitous act that sets the affairs of the novel in motion. Under pressure from Calvert's father (who interprets his son's spontaneous gesture as a response to corrupting affection), the prudish, stuffy town raises its hackles, Cotery loses his job and also a scholarship at the local college, and George Passant (the central figure of this first volume) falls into bad odor by defending Cotery against slanderous charges.

Calvert's brilliant, erratic career is not considered in detail until *The Light and the Dark* where the skeletal sketch of the earlier book is substantially fleshed out. The elaborate research that has gone into tracing Cotery's lineage (engraved on the cigarette case) is now directed toward the arcana of Sogdian; his erotic nature finds its outlet in debauchery; his fatalistic charm and preoccupation with doom are reflected in a passion for life (the "light") and a hopeless, inexplicable fascination for death (the "dark").

The Light and the Dark (as well as *The Masters* after it) comes closest to suggesting what each novel in the series should be and what it should do for the sequence as a whole. It explores in "width and depth" several important themes while showing their individual and universal applications. For one thing the novel is about faith —or rather the betrayal of faith in love, religion, and politics; for another it is about choice—choice that ostensibly evolves freely but is already determined. Snow, like any rationalistic or naturalistic writer worth his salt, accepts fate as the consequence of character as well as the other way around. But in his peculiar, and vulnerable, double role as scientist-historian he chooses to play off the essential man against environmental power complexes and predestined events; his characters are subjected to a scientific no less than historic determinism.

The essence of our nature [Eliot writes of Calvert] lay within us, untouchable by our own hands or any other's, by any chance of things or persons, from the cradle to the grave. But what it drove us to in action, the accrual of events of our lives—those were affected by a million things, by sheer chance, by the intervention of others, by the choice of our own will. So between essence and chance and will, Roy had, like the rest of us, had to live his life.[7]

When Snow is able to turn forbidding complexities like these into considerations of themes and character he is supreme. Calvert's search for faith (both moral and theological) and his various choices form the alternating light and dark episodes of a novel often overburdened by contrived complements of symbolism, but withal a total study of morbidity, sexuality, and manic depression. Whether seen at the crest of his academic career, in confidences with Eliot, in his flirtation with Nazism before the war or his service during it, Calvert is plunged into quests that are continually resolved by loss of faith and exhausted by choice. "All men are swine" (one of Calvert's final asseverations) bespeaks a misanthropy consistent with an intellectual and spiritual Manichaeism that replaces hope by fear, love by power, action by attrition.

Infected by a supernal melancholy that at last eclipses its brilliance, such a tragically fated life and its writhings after faith provide the perfect grist to Snow's mill and reflect the certitude of his historic process. In the Snovian universe of essences, Calvert emerges an existentialist whose contradictory nature, fears, and hang-ups are at variance with action. Curiously the novel may almost be construed as a morality play on failed success and the evils of genius—a contemporary *De Cassibus*, removed from theology but given a like moral twist.

As underwritten by Snow, Calvert's tragedy is the inability to make any of his choices seem reasonable in a seemingly reasonable world. Choice is a directing, a settling, a getting things done and getting on with the show. Doubt is never discounted in Snow's scheme, but it cannot remain forever fixed; it should lead to compromise and resolution, not more doubt. Whether one does the right thing for the wrong reason or vice versa is superfluous, since the belief that choice, once made, must *mean* something is perhaps more important than the actual choice itself. Martineau's decision in *Strangers and Brothers* to become an itinerant mystic; Passant's commitment in the same novel to stick by the worthless Cotery; Charles March's in *The Conscience of the Rich* to balk his father and the Jewish "crowd"; Luke's in *The New Men* to work on the bomb; and, finally, Eliot's in *The Affair* to take on Howard's case all equally imply Snow's positive (if limited) belief in the necessity for action, and in rational human beings ultimately acting and choosing effectively, though not necessarily wisely.

Entrenchment in the moral certitude of events is the premise of the entire sequence. It is also stuff for a working dialectic. Riddled though *Strangers and Brothers* is with negativisms, it continually moves toward affirmation of political, social, and intellectual control in a world where, according to Snow, problems do not increase so much in scope as magnitude, and where the future, with retrospective benevolence and sagacity, can generally understand and encompass the past. Perhaps no one has been so publicly optimistic since Tennyson, who could also subsume personal doubts and bêtes noirs of existence in hope. Significantly it is Sheila Knight (later Sheila Eliot), like Roy Calvert dark, divided, and tortured, and in the end a suicide, who affirms "belief in joy," and sparks Eliot's own "stubborn and untiring hope"—those peaks of bright prospect that look down into valleys of pessimism and despair.

Success, happiness, love, strength of character, definition of purpose, healed wounds, a rationale of life, and, above all else, the discovery of truth unfold throughout the sequence in ways that highlight the peaks and valleys. Snow's symbol for individual, and sometimes collective, progress is the zig-zag line, representing at bottom the chaotic and irrational self, at top the controlled and rational one. "For some people the down-strokes are longer than the up, and some the reverse," Passant informs Eliot. "That's all you need to hope . . . And whatever your hopes are, they've got to be founded in something like the truth." [8]

The quest for truth becomes much of the *raison d'être* for Lewis Eliot's appearance in *Strangers and Brothers*. Eliot, whether as a raw youth of great potential and scant opportunity, or as a man of good will and affairs, who has wooed and won success, persists in being "touched by hope." Snow's more tolerable (and least forced) efforts at reaching the core of Eliot and moving the moral argument of the sequence are these confrontations with truth. Here Snow's naturalism seems almost gainly. Truth does not necessarily burst upon us with shattering éclat as in Durrell, undergo subjective shifting and continual refinements as in Powell, or even come lumbering on accompanied by psychological machinery as in Mrs. Lessing. Snow's way into truth is through insight.

Unquestionably truth makes ground over the series, transforming from time to time Eliot's hopes and ideals. Acquaintance with the fraud committed by Passant and Cotery through a reading of Passant's diaries (*Strangers and Brothers*), the painfully gradual discovery of Sheila's mental condition (*Homecoming*), the intelligence of Nightingale's framing of Howard (*The Affair*), and the ultimate vision into Calvert's skeptical, driven self are Eliot's particular insights, setting the mold for his moral evaluations, and having an overall relevance for the sequence. Like so many of us, Eliot, who has spent his life "in the search for truth, of the truth about personalities, about the natures of those around [him]," who believes he can "take the truth about any human being," finds at the dead center of reckoning that he would rather "sacrifice" and "lose such insights" than smart from their lesions.[9]

Eliot's reaction (the response, in fact, of a normal, moral man to an impossible condition imposed by life) is probably weightier than a sequence overburdened by countless thematic variations on problems of morality—the sifting of conscience, the limiting of freedom, the nature of faith, the manipulation of justice, the uses and abuses of power—readily suggests. Truth quite likely gathers all things to it; it can no longer be for our day and age universal, but neither is it abstract; it is, for Snow, apodictic, given history as the quantum.

In *Corridors of Power* Eliot ruminates on his lost ideals, the mistakes of the past, and beyond both, the profit derived from uncovering error. His outlook here is riper; also, it is more discriminating and complete. Concern for events out of reach and for new events just swimming into ken—and quite naturally cognizance of opportunities for new ideals, new mistakes, new profit—openly gives the stamp of approval to history: not to its inevitability, from which there is no escape, but to its credibility. One does not simply draw truth from the past but one imposes truth upon it. The roll call of the dead in the second chapter of *The Affair*—"Despard Smith, *dead*, Eustace Pilbrow, *dead*, Chrystal, *dead*, Roy Calvert, *dead*"—the naming of the very men, in fact, who sixteen years earlier had been the vital, conflicting, violent forces of *The Masters*, shows the insight toward which all other insights yearn. Today's agonies and crises of truth become tomorrow's platitudes. Truth, then, for Snow, is never absolute, hardly even relative, only historic.

Here is a reducible logic that may explain why most

of the novels in the sequence, though ending either in defeat, frustration, or tragedy—rarely, that is, in anything "hopeful" or "positive"—are, nevertheless, hopeful and positive; and why Eliot's professional stoicism borders dangerously on Panglossianism. *Strangers and Brothers* does not profess that "all is for the best in this, the best of all possible worlds." But if the "new men"—those who have conscientiously arrived at truth by manipulating, at the same time heeding, history—do not represent the best world, at present, Snow cannot imagine a better one.

Snow's "new men" (Martin and Lewis Eliot, Walter Luke, Charles March), despite their integrity, morality, and conscience, despite their intellectual and/or social rebellion against the arch-reactionaries (Leonard March, the elder Calvert, Hector Rose), are at bottom conservative revisionists. Their rebellion for the most part proceeds cautiously, even (perhaps owing to Snow's bias) scientifically: alternatives weighed and balanced; movements calibrated; choices equated; decisions modified; results measured. In the last analysis, everything of permanence becomes an exponent of logic, place, degree. No character, for example, is really an eccentric, just as none is an "original"; and the "mad" (Sheila Eliot, Roy Calvert) either die or commit suicide.

Other moralists, like Melville, Lawrence, Camus, Faulkner, or Golding, in the fullness of their art and the inhospitality of their vision, have taught us to view the world otherwise. Order proceeds eventually from chaos, ripeness from sterility, good (or potential good) from injustice. They have shown us how man, beginning in wonder, may move on to joy through blackness, or to blackness through joy; that life, in order to be intense, must proceed irrationally, no matter what the end. This is modern man's vitality, what Snow's "new men" vitiate through an insistence that life, because it is governed by rational processes, must always unfold rationally by design.

Passant's zig-zag (ordaining a somewhat freer movement through history) would seem to the contrary. But the problem is one of time even more than of history. Snow's overall technical fallacy arises from forcing time and man to move together concomitantly and contingently, from patterning, in other words, the temporal advance upon the psychological one. Time, which is fluid—as opposed to man's progress through it which, whether rational or irrational, is anything but—cannot work this way. A temporal line may steadily rise (Mrs. Lessing), or fall (Burgess), run forward or backward singly (Powell), or as one of a number of parallel lines (Durrell), but that it can be made to zig-zag with any artistic effectiveness is unlikely. The picture of Snow, however, armed with a stopwatch, clocking the movements of his characters is, on any count, unique. He lets the second hand run around to a point; stops it; clicks it back to zero; and then lets it run around again. His use of overlapping scenes—scenes from one novel duplicated with slight variation in another—partly justifies the analogy, as does the order of the sequence. Taking the novels chronologically by publication date and correspondingly plotting on a graph the years they cover will produce the anticipated zig-zag peaks and valleys.

This erratic charting of time poses a double jeopardy: the writer fails to develop character, and subsumes it within a shaky superstructure. Snow's characters have justifiably, if somewhat harshly, been labeled flat, dull, lifeless, two-dimensional, and so forth. With the few important exceptions of Charles March, George Passant, Sheila Knight, and Eliot himself, and at least the one notable exception of Roy Calvert, this is quite true; they are jerked through the sequence like so many puppets to fulfill narratorial obligations. Casual in the mechanics of *mise en scène,* Snow becomes distressingly callous immediately his personae shuffle or collapse into the wings. When they appear again they are revived and full-blown; but what has happened in the interim in their movements from peak to valley is never clarified, nor does it even seem relevant. Faces presented upon initial entrances are identical to those prepared for exeunts, unaffected by change or time.

What can be said of the narrator in *Strangers and Brothers* is true of everyone else. Like Eliot, they all feel the lapse of time, without possessing additionally the heightened awareness that time has touched anything in passing. Almost osmotically time seeps through and away from them; they become absorbed by and into it. While Snow rightly shies from such set pieces on *ubi sunt* and mutability that mar Durrell's *Quartet,* he settles instead for the banalities of intuiting the lapse of time. One must, especially in a sequence that leaps radically from interval to interval, at some point along the way intercept time in the lists at full tilt. For Mr. Knight (Sheila's father) even in his grief to weigh with sage gravity leaden truisms ("Time heals all wounds except the passing of time"); or for Eliot to gloss the pathos of Leonard March's baronial decline by an equally rigid thesis ("Time did not matter, something which happened fifty years ago suggested something which happened yesterday"), presumes a unilateral and simplistic pact with ideas of inevitability and recurrence.

Despite their comforting portentousness—and whether Snow or his characters are intransigent is another disturbing feature of the sequence—statements like these might be taken for specimens of satire and irony were the author a satiric or ironic man. Half-truths and epigrams that stitch together the moral fabric of real life are not successful, per se, in binding the seams of fiction, since one generally reads novels not to see why things remain the same, but why they do not. It is novelistic prerogative, perhaps a feat, to render continuance without the counterpoise of change. But Snow, or any novelist interested in reduplicating dimensions rather than merely shifting perspective, is obliged to bring the techniques of variation to bear upon the idea of change: as an actor, say, portraying a bored character on stage must be continually bored with energy.

In *Strangers and Brothers* we too often feel the boredom without the energy through witnessing combinations of events and contingencies of characters that dutifully trudge on toward recurrence. Thus *Homecoming,* carrying Eliot through two marriages, two major crises, and three "homecomings" (the American title) is predictable and fatiguing in its pleonasm. And *Corridors of Power* and *The Affair*—differences in theme notwithstanding—basically backtrack over ground trodden in *The Masters,* becoming, insofar as their technique and handling of time is concerned, tautologous to the earlier work and to each other. While an essential naturalism and a fine historic sense possessed by Snow would seem to compel an ethos of change, his characters do little more than leisurely relive and reiterate the events of the past.

All this is in a way rather surprising since Snow has more than once catechized us about the novelist's responsibility in recording and reflecting change. Proust, one of his favorite authors, has entered often into his criticism and fiction, and notably been singled out as the champion who "widened the range of the novel." [10] Proust, penetrating more deeply from novel to novel into the eccentricities and subconscious of his characters and narrator, nevertheless wrought an incredible marvel by creating the illusion of limitless time and a vast, open-ended French society. Snow, for all the ostensible panoramic range and sweep of his sequence, only grows more inverted, circumscribes his society, works continually in confined, selective, areas.

But comparisons with Proust aside, Snow, even among his contemporaries, has been the most reticent to suggest precisely what changes his sequence, covering fifty-odd years, reflects. There is no sense of a shifting or decaying society as in *The Music of Time*, of fluctuating commitments as in *Children of Violence*, of an entity like the "city" as in the *Alexandria Quartet*, or of "culture" as in the *Balkan Trilogy*. Doris Lessing may often prove tedious in mirroring the slightest intellectual variation undergone by Martha Quest; Powell, mannered and distressing, often finicky in rendering nuances of alteration in the class system; Durrell, labored and overly poetic in delivering Alexandria from time; Burgess, casual and impressionistic in showing the crumbling of small section of a waning empire; but all such changes are patterned on a direction the sequences are taking and on the progression of character and action.

Change, like time, becomes in Snow's sequence a regulatable phenomenon, independent of the many strangers and brothers, and, in the last analysis, never metaphysically freed from but instead shackled to the immediate problem at hand. Snow attempts continuity for the series by modulating the nature of the issues his characters confront rather than showing change within the characters themselves. And since any abstraction like truth, justice, freedom, happiness, and so forth, must, within a civilized, conventional framework, alter quantitatively or directionally—not qualitatively on any count—Snow gives us a candid, if limited picture of how change works in individual volumes, never throughout the series as a whole. Though altering characters, setting, time, method, and the crucial "affair," Snow has written not a novel sequence so much as a sequence comprised of the same novel.

The Masters may best bear out these generalizations. Being a good story told well, filled with heightened character sketches and expectations, better paced and more compelling as a novel than the majority of volumes, it is a tight, controlled, even artistic work, most amenable to criticism. It is a novel of committee rooms, lounges, and flats, all heavy with cigar smoke, port, and high-pressure dialogue delivered in a low key. Like other novels of *Strangers and Brothers* it is an interior piece—a confidential walk is the only bit of outside leisure Snow ever permits his endomorphic intellects—but it manages a surprising range owing to the broad base upon which changes pyramid. Artistically *The Masters* is something of a tour de force. Within the small world and walls of a university is crystallized the loose and general concern for change that Snow sets sprawling over the nearly four thousand pages of the series.

The scrimmage among thirteen Fellows over the election of a new Master for their (nameless) Cambridge college is, as might be expected, symbolic of the struggle in the world at large over abstract questions of political morality, questions ultimately resolved through practical exercises in will and power. Who will win the Mastership has immediate but superficial interest; the kinds of power hungered after by the concerned parties and the power exercised in winning the election, has more. But by the time all wheedling, threatening, humiliating, arbitrating, backbiting, and jockeying have run their course, the election come and gone, and Paul Jago the loser to Thomas Crawford by the slimmest margin allowable in accord with the university's by-laws (and Snow's dramatic down-to-the-wire finish), suspense has long past, and the variations on power complexes been faithfully and predictably played out.

What of permanent distinction remains in *The Masters* is less the variation on the kinds of power that exist in the world, than the multileveled views of the changes power produces. Power's emotional effect—how it grasps, diverts, twists, frustrates, corrupts, or ruins—is fascinating, but often beyond Snow's powers as a novelist. Far better treated is the effect of power on almost the minute-by-minute shifts in thought of one Fellow or another, changes that Snow has expertly traced in men temperamentally so dissimilar as the confident, unshakable Crawford, the bitterly frustrated Nightingale, the childlike Gay, or Eliot himself, grown sager, less spontaneous, more guarded. One looks into *The Masters* as into a transparent gear case; the wheels grind on until a one-sided pressure creates stoppage of the works, to be set going again only by pressure from another side. And through Snow's near-mathematical exactitude in showing how the cogs touch at every point—in constructing his novel, that is, so that each scene contains a different complement of characters, a potentially new interaction or alignment of Fellows, a fresh perspective on both the means and the ends of the election—one looks beyond the complex assembly to the mainspring of change that turns these wheels-within-wheels.

All change in *Strangers and Brothers* is given retrospective sanction through the exercise of intellect. In *The Masters* (as elsewhere) is imposed upon reason the burden of refining, chastening, and cooling whatever emotions Snow's characters summon. (The "inner design" of the sequence, one remembers, is the resonance between what Eliot sees and what he feels.) Snow's exhaustive faith in special functions of knowledge, and his belief in cyclical "eternal recurrence" is Nietzsche without tears. Eras, like men, must die. The elegiac note struck in *Last Things*, for example, harmonizes with the prophetic realization that men of Eliot's—and Snow's—generation may be at "the end of a line." Having striven for a good and just world, they would pass on the mantle to the cream of the newer generation who will strive for a more just, better one—committing, perhaps, as many errors, but probably achieving as many successes. Thus, less interested in where things have gone than in where they are going, Snow brings the series full circle by having Eliot's son, Charles—as revolutionary, religious, modest, direct, and free as Dad is liberal, free-thinking, prideful, facetious, and bound—sever the easy and familiar ties and set out on his own.

Charles, however individualistic, is also a model of reason, and balance is all. Snow's assurance is Aristotelian: only reason can ethically control our actions, absorb change, and guide us down the via media to what passes for happiness in the complex modern world. So Aristotelian melioration vis-à-vis Nietzschean individualism makes for the dynamics of a kinetic, viable world, but also for tense, often impossible classifications. ("I like imagination rather than ordinariness," Eliot tells Francis Getliffe in *The Masters* and proceeds to settle into stodge.) Thus one is forced repeatedly to revise old, create new categories for emotion and thought. Snow is pressing the basic distinction in *Strangers and Brothers* between the intellect of emotions (Nietzsche's "knowledge is power") and the purer scientific intellect of Aristotle. Since emotions in Snow prove dangerous and destructive at every point, Aristotelian self-control is preferred to Nietzschean extremism, though both ethical systems require supermen of sorts.

While Eliot embraces change all along—as Darley, say, in the *Alexandria Quartet*, rejects it to the very end —pure thought conflicting with emotional thought (i.e., memory) forces inconsistencies within both Eliot and the sequence, due, in large measure, to Snow's own vacillation on how feeling and intellect are best reconciliable through time—no mean problem certainly. At one point in the series Eliot has a tearfully euphoric epiphany concerning the similarities between his dead wife, Sheila, and his future wife, Margaret:

> Cheated by memory, I was transported to those times —which had in historical fact been negligible in the length of our marriage—when Sheila, less earthbound than I was, had lifted me off the earth. Created by memory, I had sometimes had that mirage-joy, that false-past, shine above a happy time with Margaret, so that happiness turned heavy.[11]

Memory, here performing a shell game, later becomes less capricious and more stable. Brooding over the confrontation that has arisen between him and an old friend because of the college election, Eliot reflects in *The Masters*:

> I remembered a May week five years before, on just such a night as this, [when] there had been delight to spare for our friends. Yet, a few minutes past, I had said goodnight . . . with no intimacy at all. Was it only this conflict between us? Or was it a sign of something inevitable, like the passing of time itself? The memory of anyone one had truly loved stayed distinct always and with a special fragrance, quite unaffected by the years. And the memory of one's deepest friendships had a touch of the same magic. But nothing less was invulnerable to time, or chance, or one's private troubles.[12]

Snow's undefined drifting over ways of perceiving change is made further anomalous in *Corridors of Power*. Eliot, older, wiser, entrenched in the Establishment but nevertheless undergoing a security check owing to involvement in nuclear policies, can announce with civil fury to his interrogator that he was never "emotional about the operations of politics [and power] . . . but about the hopes behind them." Eliot, distrusting emotions because they distort, advocates a falling back on "codes of honour and behaviour," failing somehow to see that they are equally suspect.

Self-irony on Eliot's part (or laxity on Snow's) aside, change, like the men who experience it, works through such a rationalization of emotions, a coming to grips with processes on any level (love, friendship, politics), and the recognition that there must be some measure of irrevocability to the course of any life. Eliot's outburst in *Corridors of Power* is (not coincidentally) found in the section entitled "Towards a Choice." The choice in question is not exclusively Eliot's, though to remain in the civil service amidst disruption and relative insult might well be. Rather it is Roger Quaife's (an up-and-coming politician being groomed for a high-level ministry post by the Conservatives) whose "white paper" arguing for England's withdrawal in the arms race has been hostilely received by press and constituents alike. At the risk of his career—which indeed does later crumble in a vote of nonconfidence—Quaife, unpolitically, emotionally, but with incredible rectitude, pursues his obsession. His choice is complex, disastrous, immutable, but highly moral; and Quaife himself is an example of the extraordinary person who fails because he refuses to follow the path of least resistance and bucks change rather than rolls with it.

Single and decisive, Quaife's commitment is, by the standards of the world at large, more far reaching than Jago's vacillatory gestures in *The Masters*, though here the day-to-day, moment-by-moment influence of change on choice is more convincing. Quaife, in the face of all, remains stolid. To watch the very sound Jago become alternately an egotistic, erratic, volatile, subservient, possessed human being is to feel something of the charge generated by choices that are subjectively terrifying, but objectively merely mechanical and normal. Snow's particular view of choice is not the existentialist's. Rather than dwelling upon that extraordinary philosophy of existence that glorifies the *act*, but invalidates the actual *fact* of choice, Snow does a complete about-face, emphasizing what is psychologically and essentially true for most of us, while at the same time banal. Buffeted as we are by change, we are unable to embrace all choices necessary to meet it; we find, in fact, that choices become, if anything, delimiting. In Snow's fictional world, as in our real world, one is emotionally and intellectually saddled with alternatives that cannot be met by something so obvious as the conditional. "If," cries Jago after realizing that he has lost Nightingale's vote, "I'd offered him the tutorship it would have held him. . . . If I could only have made something like a promise." To which Chrystal sternly replies: "Jago, if you had promised that man the tutorship, you might have gained one vote —but you would have lost six others." [13] How very different, this view, in its comprehensiveness, its concreteness, in its affirmation of the ultimate demand on the importance of any single choice, from the final, troubled conclusion that tumbles from the still simmering brain of Camus's stranger:

> I'd passed my life in a certain way, and I might have passed it in a different way, if I'd felt like it. I'd acted thus, and I hadn't acted otherwise; I hadn't done *x*, whereas I had done *y* or *z*. And what did that mean? . . . Nothing, nothing had the least importance.

Meursault's defiant surrender to the "benign indifference of the universe" is a surrender most of us are ill prepared to make. As Snow well knows, the most insignificant things in life, everything in fact, has enormous importance when man moves, thinks, and functions as a public, rather than private being. Hence Chrystal, who by no stretch of the imagination approaches the complexity of Meursault, nevertheless heads off the stranger's and Jago's problem through a timely but dangerous logic. Rational solutions in the face of change, in the face of choice, provide ready answers, but foster a spurious acquiescence to events by making them appear governable by Reason alone, who, like the whore she is, truncates, stifles, and aborts experience. Little wonder that Lewis Eliot, pinned down over eleven volumes by a murderous crossfire of reason, is a creature with all passion spent. Snow's characters in general, though they are not overly smug, prudish, stupid, or unfeeling, are men and women of etiolated emotions, those who have learned to retrench their passions, to dig in and reason themselves into reasonable positions. Logic and intellect provide the folly of being momentarily comforted, and time rights all as one grows older.

The lesson of *The Masters* is central both to *Strangers and Brothers* and to Snow's theories of change. It teaches us that the new men of sound mind and controlled affections, guided by codes of "honour and behaviour," a stern morality, and a near-devout belief in the validity of their position relative to others, can effectively force an internal reconciliation with the externals of change. What bolsters these men from within is their ability to understand, categorize, and formulate what is happening without. "Facts" or "things" are of paramount importance in a Snow novel because on these hang the visible signs of change. In *The Affair* the "direction of time's arrow" can be charted (according to Crawford) by the "disappearance of [upper-class] privilege," just as in *The Masters* the events of a year are focused and contained in the moment of the election, and in *Corridors of Power* in Quaife's resignation.

The Masters suggests, too, somewhat dismayingly, but less ironically than one could wish, that little fruitful comes from the strife and chicanery sewn by behind-scenes politicking, that while this may personally affect people, it scarcely nudges the status quo. The situation at the end of *The Masters* differs little from that at the beginning. In the course of the novel something has bubbled to the surface, only to have subsided. The election of Crawford, however unpalatable, has been concluded and sanctioned, and Jago makes the grand (at the same time sane and reasonable) gesture by inviting the new master to dinner.

Jago, no isolated phenomenon in *Strangers and Brothers*, provides the palpable example of the supercivilization and utilitarianism that Snow's second-level heroes uphold during moments of crises. It is all very right— and all very depressing. Right, because it is the way of the world; depressing, because these men of infinite patience and superior conscience are ultimately men conservative and mediocre. Stoicism here is taken as a kind of intellectual masochism that goes to any lengths to avert threats to personal status or the security of the group. Such a symbol of discord is the bishop in *The Masters*, and, on an ascending plane, mental illness in *Time of Hope*, communism in *The Conscience of the Rich*, the atomic bomb in *The New Men*, murder in *The Sleep of Reason*. The point is that the relatively cold and rigid Snow men insulate themselves against chaos, rather than meet it head on.

If change, then, in *Strangers and Brothers*, is the force controlling events and characters, and time the fulcrum, the affair in any single novel seesaws between chaos on the one hand, order on the other. The moral, social, and of course sensible job of Snow's handpicked committees (of whatever sort) is to reason out all sides of any problem and the human values involved, to keep the affair from falling irretrievably into chaos, or to militate against the chaos that has already occurred. The collision of reason and chaos is at apogee in *The Sleep of Reason*, a novel that in the end becomes an apotheosis of the former. Like several other titles in the sequence, *The Sleep of Reason* is blatantly problematic and intensely symbolic. The line from Goya—"the sleep of reason brings forth monsters"—relates to all levels of action, some trivial, some immediate, some universal. But whether Snow is dealing with the innocuous hang-up of the chancellor's daughter over whether she should marry a well-established theoretical physicist or Eliot's rakehell nephew, the contemplated suicide of Eliot's father-in-law, student freedom on campus, power politics in academe, the generation gap, the general state of England, or the bizarre sado-sexual murder of a young boy by two lesbians, he brings things round to the novel's central theme: man's historic, societal, personal, moral, even existential responsibilities in a world that must be controlled by reason if the world is to survive. Predictably, Eliot, having focused on all wavelengths of the complex spectrum of variations, zooms in for the ultimate analysis:

> Reason. Why had so much of our time reneged on it? Wasn't that our characteristic folly, treachery, or crime?
>
> Reason was very weak as compared with instinct. Instinct was closer to the aboriginal sea out of which we had all climbed. Reason was a precarious structure. But, if we didn't use it to understand instinct, then there was no health in us at all. . . .
>
> Put reason to sleep, and all the stronger forces were let loose. We had seen that happen in our own lifetimes. In the world: and close to us. We knew, we couldn't get out of knowing, that it meant a chance of hell.[14]

Eliot, speaking here as one of Snow's "new men," is also the Aristotelian seeking the "golden mean." Instinct unbridled produces chaos, while reason (scientific or humanistic) creates order from chaos. Snow's marriage of the two cultures on this point may not always be happy, but it is ever convenient. Both scientist and humanist are builders and solidifiers; both understand the working of institutions, understand that personal and universal forces alike tend toward chaos, despite the outward show of order, and that the greatest responsibility any of us has is the repression of so cosmic a yearning. Morality and reasonableness of choice join with circumspection and a striving for harmony that must prevail if the world, exposed continually to annihilation, and the individual, undergoing his private apocalypse, are to survive. Thus Snow's men are never pulled into the abyss. What Angus Wilson has said of Zola's sociopolitically sound heroes may be said of Snow's. In a deterministic and complex world—grown more so in the century since Zola wrote—the only kind of enlightened behavior comes from the man who "directs his own advantage in the direction in which society is moving, not [from the] fool who attempts to alter events."

No one better than Snow realizes that calculating, mechanical behavior of this sort, organized rigidly, geared to efficiency and, hopefully, perfection, goes against nature, and is gained only at the shattering expense of personality. Lawrence, in *Women in Love*, had written forty years before

> [Gerald Crich] was just ahead of them [the miners] in giving them what they wanted, this participation in a great and perfect system that subjected life to pure mathematical principles. This was a sort of freedom, the sort they really wanted. It was the first step in undoing, the first great phase of chaos, the substitution of the mechanical principle for the organic, the destruction of the organic purpose, the organic unity, and the subordination of every organic unit to the great mechanical purpose. It was pure organic disin-

tegration and pure mechanical organisation. This is the first and finest state of chaos.

Crich would be sorely out of place in the cabals and "at homes" of *Strangers and Brothers,* but his mechanistic philosophy is curiously present, pervasive.

In a century continually notorious for overt, destructive expressions of the totalitarian personality, Lawrence's fear that the "great mechanical purpose" would destroy the individual seems still unfounded, at least in the long view of things. Cybernetics, at one time the lion in the streets, now utters subdued growls in back alleys while unlicensed individualism—Black Power, White Power, Colonialism, Nationalism, Imperialism— stalks our conscience. A patient historian like Snow can gain unlimited focus from the realpolitik of the world. The *ends* in *Brave New World* are perhaps less terrifying than the *means* of avoiding them. Do we ultimately cast our lot with Orwell in 1984, with Anthony Burgess in *A Clockwork Orange,* or with Snow in *Strangers and Brothers?* For a rational humanist (and Snow *is* this) the dilemma must become obsessive, ugly, painful. How is it possible, he asks, to make the power-philosopher both the ruler and servant of mankind? Is not this "finest chaos"—chaos, incidentally, only to the extremist—more reasonable than the anarchy of individualism? At the expense of Snow's so called Byzantinism—the increased rigidity of class structure and of corporate and government enterprise, the consolidation of the tentacles of power—we have apparently lost our light, vitality, purpose. But to contain society, the nation, the world; to prevent their devolution into a chaos in *fact,* not simply in *spirit,* is the job to which Snow's new men are oriented, the difficult, almost impossible, but morally necessary one history demands of them.

Snow's perspective in *Strangers and Brothers* has

evolved from this humane, but excessively rational over-view. Conservatism and stodge are the lot of those who roll with change, rather than buck it. But even Snow's rebels, through ego or passion, out of idealism, stupidity, madness, must eventually bend to the inexorable forces that round off their lives in the series, in this fictional world which, because of its overall validity, is more un-comfortably real than we would like to think. Scientist that he is (or was), Snow, as writer, resolves our social, moral, political dilemmas by example as well as through rhetoric. Who could gripe at Eliot's self-accounting of his ambitions— "not to spend my life unknown; love: a better world?" Who would deny any man such a birth-right? Or who dare sneer at his "stubborn and untiring hope"? Eliot, in *Last Things*, redeems his type and class. Too old for passion, too worn for the power game, he falls back on what he understands best, himself, hoping for ten more years of life to devote to writing and "last things," hoping to meet death with (in Rilke's phrase) "no unlived lines in the body," but mostly, simply hop-ing. Such men of strength and purpose and hope can do us little harm, and they may even do us a great deal of good. As Snow suggests, so long as the Lewis Eliots are around to organize and synthesize, our problems may be solved (if they are to be solved at all) through com-promise and amelioration, though often at the expense of freedom.

For England and for the human race, Snow's solutions are not entirely unattractive. Through identical beliefs in the sense of order and the respect for reason, strangers may become brothers. But if Snow looks toward time, change, and history to supply the enlightened commen-tary and patterns for our codes of behavior, he also im-plies that the free-wheeling zig-zag may decline into nar-rowing, concentric circles; which is only to conclude that Snow, for all his deficiencies as an artist, is, as thinker, wrestling with the central paradox of our age. Living within a controlled society may provide the sole key to historic order, may buffet the chaotic forces of time or change. Yet is this not a terrible price to pay if individuality, freedom, and the demonic, creative, even self-destructive urge is totally absorbed into a strong, saving, uniform, but equally horrifying morality?

6

Anthony Powell
A *Dance to the Music of Time*: The Comedy of History

Two decades, nine volumes, and three quarters of a million words have raised Anthony Powell to the top rank of contemporary British writers, and his long work in progress, A *Dance to the Music of Time*, to one of the most sweeping and extraordinary sequences of the century. A work that has never relinquished surface brilliance for portraying the insular, exclusive, private, and snobbish world of the British upper and middle classes —Tory, Royalist, Anglican—has latterly become a vast canvas on all English life between the wars and afterwards, abounding in diversity and eccentricity. And, in the profoundest way, it has become no less than a comic epic on time, history, and change.

Informed by Powell's genius for comic invention, *mise en scène*, and dialogue, *The Music of Time* weaves into the shifts and changes of England's last fifty years the destiny of hero-narrator Nicholas Jenkins, upon whom falls the job of relating cause and effect, of descrying the figure in the carpet, of prodding or pressing the past into shape, and, perhaps most importantly, of growing. Son of a retired army officer, Nick moves casually through public school and the university into publishing, later into script-writing, a captaincy in the army, and most recently back into civilian life. Along this route he has good and bad love affairs, writes several novels, gets married, and continually enjoys unlimited entrance into the sophisticated echelons of England's upper classes. Through all changes—the failure and death of friends, the decline of family, the shaking of class, the fall of nations—he leisurely narrates his life and the lives of those his life intersects: a narration notably marked by a coolness that masks intense feelings running like powerful undercurrents beneath the surface.

There is at times something glacial in Nick's reserve, in the cultivated aloofness perhaps necessary for proper narrative omnipotence. Even when "involved," Nick keeps his distance and hangs in the background, more concerned with what is happening around him than to him, aware that excessive attention to his own particular steps might mar the general design of the dance, and forever propped by his comic perspective. Such a perspective, however, does not tamper with his view of history. A faithful narrator, he is no facetious historian. He accepts experience with no thought of forecasting its long-range significance. Nick reacts with sympathy, amusement, or mild astonishment to the things happening around him, for he refuses to be daunted by change and is, in the last analysis, only fascinated by it.

Proper, fashionable, sincere, self-reliant, he is the above-average, upper-class all right guy wanting to fit in and keep from becoming defeated, excessively eccentric, too notoriously successful, or too scandalously simple. These are the alternatives in *The Music of Time* for those who contribute to Nick's education. Characters whose convictions prove mistaken fall prey to delusion, while those whose perceptions have failed at the outset are assailed by illusions equally destructive. Adherents to outmoded beliefs and untenable positions, they travel toward destruction of one sort or another, taking society with them. Nick, bolstered by his attitude and primed by experience, sees the dissolution and charts a course

between extremes, measuring the smallest signs or gestures against contemporary standards and holding fast
to sensible and humane values. From his shadowy beginnings as narrator and his often obvious role as author-
surrogate, he has emerged into a full-blown hero; for
above and beyond other things, he has learned how a
student of history and society should confront the uses
of the past and of men.

If the past proves important in playing on the sensitivity and sensibilities of Nick, it excites no cataclysmic
revelations, but low-keyed, meaningful insights. In a
work that sets out to be both life and fiction, history
and myth, Powell strikes a balance between what has
really happened in the last fifty years and how the
novelist might view its happening. Decay, for example,
or the "disintegration of values" as Hermann Broch has
called it, is a motif of the century; it is also a leading
theme of *The Music of Time*. To the historian, such
decay may emerge as a single, simple fact, as, say, the
fall of any empire is a fact. The totalities involved in
accounting for it, however, are never as factual or as
simple as one might like them to be. The historian may
see decay as the most contributive factor of change. The
novelist—Powell in this case—knows that it is only one
part of change; growth is another, individual growth that
is rarely accounted for in the historic process and is often
lost in the indifference and inexorability of time.

Still, Nick moves with time and history, not against
them. He is neither the dupe of events, the sport of fate,
nor merely the ingenious persona of a superior intelligence. Seldom a rootless or alienated factor in such political or social equations that loom larger than himself,
he is most often the normative, sane link between what
at first seems dissonant or disparate and what eventually
—*when*, no one knows—makes sense. The "epiphany,"
the illumination, the *Augenblick*—that flashing, tran-

sient, pure vision within the dark and muddled flux of *temps perdu*—is not for him. He simply measures the pace necessary to the moment—the importance of which may escape him, may be of little or much significance, may be uncertain, but which is as just and logical at the particular instant as any other single moment. As a passable, but youthful philosopher, Nick can observe toward the end of *A Buyer's Market* that "action, built up from innumerable causes, each in itself allusive and unnoticed . . . is almost always provided with an apparently ideal moment for its final expression." [1] But as a mature novelist, Powell is not interested in what sort of patterns time and history make, only that it makes them. Nothing, for example, can be drawn from Nick's recapitulation in *The Acceptance World* of the chain of events that has inadvertently developed into his liaison with Jean Templer, his mistress.

> I had enacted such scenes with Jean: Templer with Mona: now Mona was enacting them with Quiggin: Barnby and Umfraville with Anne Stepney: Stringham with her sister Peggy: Peggy now in the arms of her cousin: Uncle Giles, very probably with Mrs. Erdleigh: Mrs. Erdleigh with Jimmy Stripling: Jimmy Stripling, if it came to that, with Jean: and Duport, too. [2]

The observation is complete in itself, a pure synthesis of situation, what has been actual, as well as necessary, in the movement of time to bring things to where they stand at present.

How this sense of the present works throughout the sequence is one of its distinguishing features. Like most modern novels that lack a beginning or middle or end, *The Music of Time* creates its ambience out of continuing change. But what Powell does with the notion is unique. By seeing all possible, movable, interchangeable patterns, but by placing the burden of interpreting them squarely on his narrator, he makes the present the exclusive and solid center of the novel, and thrusts the past, i.e., "lost time," "history," outward toward the peripheries. This method—for Powell wittily toys again and again with design and variation—enlarges even the most underplayed gestures without focusing on their immediate significance. The general premise of the other sequences, that the past is somehow inimical and casts a long shadow into the future, brings about the tragic overview of man struggling in the face of time. Durrell, for example, sets about to deliver time; Mrs. Lessing to overcome it; Snow to justify it; Mrs. Manning to crystallize it as permanence; Burgess to absorb it. Powell passively accepts its movement, his object being the integration of individual actions into the greater flux, while simultaneously playing changing sensibilities against the continuum of human history. In such harmony of movement—the word "movement" pertinent in its musical, mechanical, and recently even its military sense—is resolved the comic view of life that refuses to see characters overwhelmed by the backdrop of change (the tragic implication once again), but rather conjoined and moving with it, a view contained both literally and metaphorically in the dominant symbol of the sequence—the dance.

The opening of the first novel, A *Question of Upbringing*, depicts a group of workmen warming themselves over a coke stove on a wintry English evening.

The physical attitudes of the men themselves as they turned from the fire suddenly suggested Poussin's scene in which the seasons, hand in hand and facing outward, tread in rhythm to the notes of the lyre that the winged and naked greybeard plays. The image of Time brought thoughts of mortality: of human beings facing outward like the Seasons, moving hand in hand in intricate measure: stepping slowly, methodically, sometimes a trifle awkwardly, in evolutions that take recognisable shape: or breaking into seemingly meaningless gyrations, while partners disappear only to reappear again, once more giving pattern to the spectacle: unable to control the melody, unable, perhaps, to control the steps of the dance.[3]

This striking simile—simplifying in a few lines the actual technique of the sequence, yet compounding seemingly inexhaustible complexities of character by-play—has picked up broader implications and richer contexts since its appearance nearly twenty years ago. On the surface it of course attempts to capture the sometimes fortuitous, sometimes planned rhythms of humanity itself. Moving *in* time, never static, Powell's characters align and realign themselves, define and redefine relationships. Such alignments and definitions can be measured at once, but not at the moment understood, just as one might grasp the individual figures and gestures in Poussin's painting without immediately recognizing the tension and drama at work within the closed world he creates.

But there is, too, the attendant and equally important movement *of* time: its qualitative rather than quantitative function, the "thing-in-itself" that makes one "unable . . . to control the steps of the dance." With good reason Nick can say (as he does in *The Kindly Ones*) that "time can play within its own folds, tricks that emphasise the insecurity of those who trust themselves over much to that treacherous concept." [4] The prime mover that does not ostensibly move—in a sequence continually reshaping the dance—*does* move, itself become part of a "kaleidoscope, the colours of which are always changing, always the same." Thus, this movement *of* and *in* time creates new patterns of the dance that succeed, but do not supersede, the older patterns, for the movement is never strictly linear. The richness of the novel does not come merely from reworking character, theme, or action in a different light, but from transposing or displacing them, gaining almost a vertical lift in construction.

There is a consistency to such method, though a witty work like *The Music of Time* never bogs down in the creaky machinery of theory. Very much in keeping with Powell's comic and ironic purposes, things move steadily along on the horizontal plane while subtly and integrally modulating vertically.

As an example of how this works with character, one might best follow the onward and upward progress of Kenneth Widmerpool, the most notorious, vital, and original creation in the sequence, and certainly one of the great contemporary comic villains. Linearly, Widmerpool has advanced from the arch-butt of his school fellows to a highly competent businessman, army colonel, and undoubtedly before the sequence is completed, an influential figure in the postwar Labor Government. Like some ominous, lumbering, insensate machine, Widmerpool moves uninterruptedly and unfeelingly toward success. His change from a bit of a pig to a total swine might conceivably bespeak hierarchical ascent. Certainly his supercompetence, speciousness, insensitivity, and increasing lack of humanity have made him the perfect foil for Nick's emergent decency, dignity, and probity—not to mention the complicated interplay with the dozens of other characters with whom he comes in contact. But perhaps most importantly for the modulating effect, Widmerpool is so involved in the configuration of historic events that there is often the odd feeling that it is he who propels them, becoming—without any overt symbolism—a bodily extension of the historic moment.

Widmerpool, whatever reversals he experiences as a person, as a force harmonizes with the *Zeitgeist* when not actually running one step ahead of it. If, as remarked above, Nick moves with time and history, it is by way of a passive acceptance and a comic stoicism of which (one imagines) Powell approves. Widmerpool's engagement with time and history is an active encounter, in such a way that they seem to move with him, to be incorporated in his larger-than-life character. It is the Widmerpool of *A Buyer's Market* who, in the height of the depression, makes out by taking calculated but sound risks; it is the Widmerpool of *The Kindly Ones* who bursts in upon Sir Magnus Donners's *dolce vita* charades; bulky, uniformed, sober, "a sinister figure calling the world to arms"; it is the Widmerpool of the war trilogy who invokes the "Rules and Discipline of War" even to the destruction—perhaps murder—of Charles Stringham and Peter Templer; and it is the Widmerpool of *The Music of Time* who has monstrously swelled from "a fish recently hauled from the water" to an increasingly less comic leviathan gobbling up the little lives of the floundering upper classes.

However remarkable a creation, Widmerpool—like the many other characters, like Nick himself—fits into those larger thematic patterns that in their turn are related and subordinated to the dominant motif weaving in and out, horizontally and vertically, through the sequence. Whether outlining the tortuous configurations of love (as in *The Acceptance World*), painting the eccentricities of class (as in *At Lady Molly's*), demarcating the limits of decay in marriage (as in *Casanova's Chinese Restaurant*), or (as in all three novels comprising the "war trilogy") dramatizing difficulties of remaining human in the face of dangerous and impersonal dehumanizing processes, Powell builds his analyses upon a dualism fundamental to human nature, yet peculiarly symptomatic of the twentieth century: a dualism that sets in opposition the man of will and the man of imagination, the power-hungry and the sensualist.

Emerging as an almost full-blown prototype in the person of Widmerpool, the man of will moves through *The Music of Time*, now as J. G. Quiggin, now as Mark Members, Ralph Barnby, Commander Foxe, Idwal Kedward; originating in Stringham, the man of imagination becomes now Uncle Giles, now Edgar Deacon, Hugh Moreland, Rowland Gwatkin, or often Nick himself. Their clash, direct or indirect, ideological or personal, comic or tragic, sustains the tension among characters, triggers the action, provides the overall suspense. Caught up in a vastly changing, complex world, the men of imagination are often paralyzed, ever magnetized by their own predicament and by the force of will—the men of power who work the changes.

These progressive, surprising, but generally logical changes, while carrying one novel sequentially beyond another, also make it the apogee of what has gone before. The uncovering of new attitudes and attributes for the men of will and imagination—the piling on, so to speak, of different levels of character that influence theme and are in turn influenced by it—accounts for the strength of Powell's vertical lift in time. Through accumulation and accretion of fragment upon fragment, one comes closest to a comprehensive view of Powell's "types"; the genus is revealed by way of the species, and vice versa. One knows Widmerpool for himself or as a man of will by his actions offstage as well as on. Reappearing as a principal figure in the dance after brief intervals in the wings, he has benefitted from the presence of other men of will holding the foreground in his absence. The same might be said about Stringham and the men of imagination. In either case, Powell's characters return with a redoubled vitality that reinforces the overall thematic patterning. Since *The Music of Time* (paraphrasing Arthur Mizener) forwards neither "philosophy, esthetic, ideology or moral," character and theme—more dependent upon each other as a consequence—work primarily through rich exchanges and interchanges. When in *The Soldier's Art* Nick is informed by Stringham that he "now is trying to get things straight in [his] own mind," one is made properly aware of just how tenuous the man of imagination's position in the world is. And later, at the end of *The Military Philosophers*, when Widmerpool flatly avows, "I have come to the conclusion that I enjoy power," the reverberating ironies are incredibly disproportionate to the casualness of the remark. Yet, in that particular moment is summed up all one has come to know and expect of Widmerpool; all that is terrifying and comic about his exercise of will, all that is ultimate and tragic in the pure exercise of power.

Implications like these—emerging naturally from any lengthy and complex interplay of character and theme—are further integrated into the series' action, which is played out on the two distinct levels of temporal movement. Horizontally, the sequence moves by way of a straightforward, generally unbroken chronology—there is only a single flashback of any duration [5]; vertically, it expands by duplicating or reforming in the present—perhaps with slight modifications—an action of the past. One most often sees this method invoked whenever an old acquaintance from the past turns up and Nick is charged with revaluation. But of the truly large blocks of significant action (Nick's revisiting Milly Andriadis's party in *The Acceptance World*, his roaming through the bombed-out public house at the opening of *Casanova's Chinese Restaurant*, his return after some seven years to the hotel where Uncle Giles died), perhaps the most dramatic, though as always underplayed, parallel occurs in *The Kindly Ones*.

As a boy in his home at Stonehurst, Nick grows accustomed to the eccentric cook Albert's nightly closing of the shutters against local suffragettes. The routine is aborted and Stonehurst vacated by Nick and his family in the early days of the First World War. Years later, Nick (now an over-thirty itching for a commission) waits in Lady Molly Jeavons's drawing room while her husband pins up the curtains during a London blackout. Both actions can of course be construed as symbolic ones; time and history cannot be shut out, the Furies must be engaged rather than propitiated. But the literal contexts are no less interesting. The action bridges the twenty-five years in which Nick has grown. It shifts the focus from passivity (noncomprehension, really) toward the first war to total commitment (of a sort) in matters of the second. Albert's and Ted Jeavons's gestures are more or less the same, yet are linked beyond mere cause and effect. Catastrophic social and political upheavals have intervened. The latter action, in short, without explaining the former, heightens it while becoming more substantial in and for itself. With Powell, a congruent action shared between past and present does not necessarily make the past come alive—that, says Nick at several points, is history—but gives greater weight to the present, the ethos of the sequence. Without seeming arch, one might say that all the actions of *The Music of Time* are geared to making it a "remembrance of things present."

By now it may be fairly clear that the horizontal and vertical movements of character, theme, and action are related—but never subordinated—to the controlling medium of the sequence, time. And (perhaps clearer still) Powell, in a way remarkable for a twentieth-century novelist concerned with time, chooses to view it neither philosophically, psychologically, nor scientifically. Absent is any Bergsonian mysticism that informs Proust's great sequence, the Freudian stream-of-consciousness refined in *Ulysses* and *The Sound and the Fury*, Einsteinian relativity and theories of the fourth dimension attempted in Durrell's *Quartet*. In all these cases time becomes internalized, subjected to personal ordering, as though the individual believed, perhaps rightly, that he could at last control the hitherto uncontrollable. With Proust time is intuitional; past actions are sustained in the present and the present is interpretable only in terms of the past. With Joyce and Faulkner time is splintered into bits, allowing an eternity of fragmented thoughts to flash in seconds through the subconscious. And with Durrell (though not always successfully) time extends beyond even the common, everyday temporal conscious or subconscious and appears relative to a plurality of minds through which it courses simultaneously.

For Powell, however, external time (clock time) is the flux. Time is actual; its very sheerness brings about events as it relentlessly pursues the dancers who, loving, marrying, dying, are reluctant to admit that they are changing at all. Powell returns to the classical conceptions of time: the musical old graybeard who conducts the rounds of the seasons, or the cold goddess Mutability, altering people and incidents from day to day. Consequently, time functions critically, not mystically. Passing because it must, it is not mysterious, only indefinable at moments. Powell is concerned with time, not obsessed by it; for while he sees it as blasting the hopes of some, wasting the promises of others, he accounts it the sole arbiter for shaping in the future the formless formulas of the past.

These concepts, at the center of *The Music of Time*, resound as notes of resignation, often melancholy or sad, sometimes even tragic, but mostly pitched to the comic stoicism and developing awareness of the narrator that keep the sequence from growing tedious, oppressive, or unwieldy. Nick's growth and attitude throughout the sequence—and the added realization that through the artifice of fiction he becomes his own best example—

prescribe the totally human, logical, and balanced perspective on the admittedly unpleasant themes of change and decay.

The primary act in Nick's genesis—and that of *The Music of Time*—begins when he is completing the upper forms of public school. Powell launches into the narrative proper by creating an atmosphere similar to that projected by the Poussin analogy. A *Question of Upbringing* complements the entire sequence by itself projecting time and space. It is concerned with shadows and foreshadowings: of the things in youth that foreshadow adulthood, of some shadows that will fade in the light of reality, of others that become reality itself. The novel opens on a dreary English day in December. Fog rolls up the valley through a thin drizzle. Kenneth Widmerpool (the loner and parvenu, chilling and omnipresent like the weather) huffs up the road, willing himself to run off excess weight; while Charles Stringham, the darling of the Establishment, almost sacrosanctly removed from external forces, warms himself within before a cozy fire.

Even at this early and amorphous stage, Powell (coupling natural and human phenomena) symbolically sketches the antitheses of personality and temperament that generate the clash of character so important to his grand design. Stringham, the man of imagination, is, one soon discovers, at odds with himself, rent internally. Widmerpool, the man of will, suffers no such ambivalence; he is machinelike in direction and certainty, outwardly a clown but inwardly whole and ordered. Such men of will and power, the mechanists, harmonize with their times; the men of imagination, the romantics, do not. Transplants from another age, they suffer "the strain of living simultaneously in two different historical periods."

Such patterns—more fluid and intricate than any critical synthesis suggests—are adumbrated as Nick measures the extremes and gauges the norms of behavior impressed upon him through the two chief influences of youth. Here is the first instance in the sequence of Powell's "theme and variation" technique that aids in creating a comparative history of the present. For as every act and gesture reflect upon upbringing, upbringing itself becomes the mirror catching images of the contrasting types who dominate Nick's world and decade.

The balances in A *Question of Upbringing* are struck among families (Nick at the Stringhams', at the Templers', at the Leroys' in France) and school (Nick at Eton, then Cambridge). In each case similarities play upon differences. While school may emphatically articulate certain youthful idiosyncracies, dreams, and ambitions, the resonances are incomplete without sounding the complex feelings and attitudes formed through family ties. The uninhibited schoolboy of the rambling countryside is seldom the same as the precise son of the drawing room. As Nick observes, "It is not easy—perhaps not even desirable—to judge other people by a consistent standard." Nick's encounters and experiences comprise, in short, a school-family syndrome—neither element can be done away with—that prepares him for society.

The threshold of this society is the university where concepts of power and sensuality mature. J. G. Quiggin (representing the turbulence and flamboyance of the will as Widmerpool exemplifies its dangers and inexorability) pulls him one way; and Uncle Giles, a muddled failure whose fruitless contentions against the world are concentrated in his hobbyhorse, "the Trust" (a vague sort of entity that brings in a moderate income) and in inveighing against lack of "influence," intrigues him the other. How the Quiggins succeed and how the Giles fail is the question concerning Nick at the close of the first volume. With the future before him, with the realization that character is fate—not upbringing nor influence —Nick knows he must fall back on himself.

The end of innocence brings with it the awareness that life must take on some sort of plan; but it is the meaning within its outlines that Nick really seeks. A *Buyer's Market* pictures him precisely at moments when he is weighing such meaning and when he is drifting from identity to identity. Nick is determined to create from post-university life an ability to function both privately and publicly; however, he often reveals an awkwardness in fusing these two selves. Logic demands a "uniformity of pattern . . . rightly preserved in human behaviour," but experience reveals that life is, on the contrary, inconsistent. At times Nick denies any design at all to human experience, retreating into solipsism; at other times he is able to reconcile the ostensible paradox of logic and experience by following connections to their ends. Running the gamut of permissible social experiences from the fashionable milieu of Eaton Square dinners and dances, to the free-for-all at Hill Street (thrown by the exotic Milly Andriadis), to the Bohemian birthday party for the artist Edgar Deacon, is quite like running around in three different interlocked circles.

Actually, the comedy of A *Buyer's Market* borrows as much from the novel's structure (the imposition of what might be called circular resistance on Nick's straightforward and straight-faced approach to his various problems) as from its related central theme: the historical, and in some ways ethical opposition of "Gothic manners" and "Greek morals," further modes of the clash between power and sensuality. Were it a question of either-or, Nick would undoubtedly abandon himself to Grecian sensuousness and simplicity. But this is hardly the case. Although a cold commercialism underlies the very foundations of modern and medieval Gothic—the abstract realities of the Middle Ages (Church and State,

Religion and Politics) replaced by those of the twentieth century (the Market, Marriage, Money) —Gothicism, too, possesses a Ruskinesque vitality found in men like Barnby, Widmerpool, Magnus-Donners, and Quiggin. Convoluted, artificial, rough, thrusting a Gothic manners are, they clearly dominate the freedom and looseness of Greek morals, the one involving willful participation, the other imaginative passivity. Half-Greek, half-Gothic in attitude, Nick seeks the best of both worlds, strives for the ideal pattern, only to endanger his decisions by lapsing into a brilliant eclecticism—a kind of fluid, confused Hellenism—which attempts to meet complexities through adaptation of old forms and development of new ones.

It is not really until the third volume of the sequence that Nick comes of age. Like the majority of Powell's titles, *The Acceptance World* is ironically literal and symbolically ironic. Explicitly, the phrase refers to Widmerpool's new occupation as a bill-broker who, "on the strength of [his] reputation," persuades banking houses to "accept" future debts for goods being shipped abroad. But since economics is not a guaranteed gauge for emotions or for life, the novel's thematic movement, and much of its comedy, depends on other kinds and degrees of "acceptance" Nick encounters as he primes himself for future responsibilities. The future, in fact, broods over the novel from the first, connecting the seemingly unrelated worlds of Mrs. Erdleigh's spirits and Widmerpool's portentous deals. Both worlds are concerned with predicting fate and ostensibly "willing" such predictions into being. And, as Nick discovers, success and acceptance depend less on interpreting the past than on manipulating the future. By this standard, Mrs. Erdleigh and Widmerpool are figures of power, though they presage different things: she, love; he, wealth. As Nick nears thirty, love and wealth emerge as the most dynamically viable symbols of his role, the yardsticks of his willingness to accept and his ability to be accepted.

The problems stated in A *Question of Upbringing* (where do you belong after being formed and fashioned by school and family?) and freely answered in A *Buyer's Market* (here, there, everywhere, nowhere, depending on who you are!) is worked out in *The Acceptance World.* Love (sensuality) and wealth (power) now become the absolutes differentiating the men of imagination and the men of will, explored through the central metaphor of "acceptance" and proceeding from the witty dialectic of thesis (the breakup of class and overall societal disintegration), antithesis (the search for patterns to aid in reconstruction), and synthesis (the acceptance of or commitment to a relationship based on love). The art and argument of *The Acceptance World* has its own geometric form, the triangle, at whose apexes the lines of tension and opposition converge. There are those triangles patterned on love (Jean Duport, her husband, Jimmy Stripling; Nick, Jean, Bob Duport; Milly Andriadis, Charles Stringham, Dicky Umfraville; Anne Stepney, Barnby, Umfraville), those patterned on power (Quiggin, Members, St. John Clarke; Widmerpool, Stringham, Le Bas; Myra Erdleigh, Giles, Stripling), and the principal love-power triangle formed by Peter Templer, Quiggin, and Mona Templer. What these antic alignments and realignments suggest to Nick is that power-in-love and love-in-power are reconcilable antinomies, for in the real sense (that is, beyond the abstract paradox) love *becomes* power; power, love. The clash of sensuality and the will is the rule in *The Music of Time* that the reader, as well as Nick, should by now have come to accept.

Opening the second trilogy, *At Lady Molly's* spans the brief period between Nick's liaison with Jean Templer Duport and his engagement to Isobel Tolland, and shows his exchanging an ambience of love without responsibilities for a world of marital preparation. Nick is still in flux and experience is still formative, but he is now, in a single word, relaxed. Now accepted and accepting, he has matured in refining impression and fact, exercising the strictest control over his role as observer and performer, wedding actuality and memory, focusing more on the present than the past. The past, however, is always viable. The leading motif of *At Lady Molly's*, settling down, emerges logically and naturally from earlier premises of acceptance to counterpoint even the eccentrics who, in one way or another, tend to be unsettling.

Eccentricity, which becomes a major subtheme in *The Music of Time*, is given its first full expansion here. Up until the fourth volume much of Powell's attention has focused on the egocentric man of will—his advent, onslaught, achievement—the circles of society in which he moves, and the man of imagination he so often bests. The dominant note throughout is a weary one; excess of either power or sensuality leads to the annihilation of the social entity. As buffers against such oppressive extremes, eccentrics have their compelling side, attractive because of their humanity and ingenuousness, and, fittingly ironic, for their balanced perceptions and eye for fine discriminations. Powell uses eccentricity to pinpoint the weaknesses of the upper classes, but not as a weakness in itself. Characters of deviation are necessary in the range of any long novel (as they are in life) for illuminating experiences or comparing them. If Powell views the aristocracy as bordering on, indeed partially undergoing, a private *Götterdammerung*, he sustains sympathy for those sinking, like their myths, into twilight. General Conyers (the eccentric pragmatist) and Erridge (the eccentric idealist) are engaging because they resist the stultifying forces of classification by ordering their own worlds. But they also appear refractory when positing philosophies—scientific, social, or otherwise—to account for the flesh-and-blood predicament in which Nick finds himself. Powell realizes how close eccentrics can come to riding a liberating fancy to the ground and pinning the human beneath the abstract.

Apart from this central idea, *At Lady Molly's*—perhaps the funniest novel in the sequence—is more decorative than functional. It makes the point of how thoroughly unsettling the business of settling down can be by easing off the masks of relationship that are, like Molly Jeavons's parties, "mixed-bags." But it is for the next chapter of the sequence to trace more deeply the faces beneath them.

Casanova's Chinese Restaurant is at once both restrained and tragic. Its subject, simply stated, is marriage; but the theme is transformed into gloomy variations on infidelity, frustration, and failure, or played against a darker passacaglia of disintegration and death. Marriage and death comprise its objective world, but ghosts haunt its ethos. The flesh-and-blood realm of *At Lady Molly's* —its party lights, brilliant eccentrics, comic relief—dissolves into the darkness of abandonment, the barrenness of the abyss. The novel is set in 1936–37 when the historic shadows of destruction are already lengthening. Events of the Spanish Revolution link the marshaling of furies in *The Kindly Ones* with the war itself in the three subsequent volumes. Franco and the rape of Spain, Hitler and the fall of Czechoslovakia, ordain the rubble and ruin of the blitzed pub (described at length in the opening paragraph) that revives in Nick memories of the previous decade. But global tragedy provides only the backdrop for the personal one. Ghosts of chaos and anarchy become incidentally important to the private, orderly ghosts summoned by Nick, and the two motifs underscoring the novel's major themes.

Powell's investigation of marriage evolves from conversational evenings in a grubby restaurant named after the immortal libertine; and preoccupation with death and infidelity (figuratively the death of marriage) is associated with an amusement-park operation called the Ghost Railway on which Nick and the composer Hugh Moreland rode in days of freedom and irresponsibility. Casanova's rogueries and amours are ironically juxtaposed with scuttled marriages; his heroism with the sorry, unheroic, pathetic figures Nick's acquaintances turn out to be in the marriage game. The railway as an image is far more direct. Its ghosts are specters of paradox. Crazily jerking through the erratic motions of a piece of vital, intricate machinery, the roller coaster is made analogous to the indeterminate, capricious, but somehow controlled functions of society

> slowly climbing sheer gradients, sweeping with frenzied speed into inky depths, turning blind corners from which black, gibbering bogeys leapt to attack, rushing headlong towards iron-studded doors, threatened by imminent collision, fingered by spectral hands, moving at last with dreadful, ever increasing momentum towards a shape that lay across the line.[6]

Such spasmodic lurching toward a vague shape—the future? change? suicide and death? war?—is the first suggestion in *The Music of Time* of an image opposing the disciplined movements of the dance whose accompaniment has plunged into a minor key with a surprising lack of transition. The dissonance and atonality of *Casanova's Chinese Restaurant* mark—with Powell's cautious respect for symbols—the dissident lives of the major characters, most of whom happen to be musicians. Fittingly, music, the memory of the sweet voice of a crippled singer, leads Nick into recollections of their crippled lives. Her song—a languorous, sentimental tale of lotus-eating narcosis, recounting escape, warmth, quiescence, beauty, exoticism—contrasts ironically with the circumscribed, cold, prosaic world of marriage; with particular focus on the marriages and careers of the rising composer, Moreland, and the music critic, Maclintick, and their respective reconstruction and ruin.

Shaggy, masculine, intense, and highly creative, Moreland finds his marital and extramarital entanglements corollaries for entanglements with his art and the times. His crises develop throughout 1936 and harbor comparisons with the Duke of Windsor's abdication: the loosing—one dislikes calling it the evading—of wider responsibilities for personal fulfilment, the break with tradition, the sacrifice of duty to love. As Moreland is "saved" by his wife, Maclintick is partially ruined by his: a ruin all the more painful and masochistic considering Maclintick's veneration of Moreland, whose character, genius, potential fame are reminders of the critic's own deficiencies. Maclintick is a dejected, lonesome, disappointed, defeated person, plagued by melancholia, frustrated by a sterile calling, destroyed first by an execrable marriage, then by his own hand. As if to exploit the sensual flaw, or to enforce the motif of "decline and fall," Powell brings Stringham back onstage—Stringham at his nadir, equally a victim of isolation and masochism, and like Maclintick an alcoholic. Maclintick's suicide is only the dramatic extension of the Stringham case. Given his values, the temperament of his wife, and the potentially destructive powers of marriage, it is totally explicable. Certain movements, as Nick comes to realize, are unalterable; there is even cause and effect at work in the weird and crazy gyrations of something like the Ghost Railway that hurtles into the dark, fateful, unfulfilled future to resurrect at the right moment the "shape [lying] across the line."

The mood of *Casanova's Chinese Restaurant* is pursued in *The Kindly Ones* as Nick, standing at yet another threshold, World War II, is harried by the Furies of history. The Eumenides have become the "shape across the line," while the permutable, protean, evasive past refuses to be shaped; or so the syllogism winnowed from the novel suggests. If the past is indeed history, and if (as patterns of recurrence seem to prove) the past is not dead, then of course history is very much alive. Though he would like to deny it, there is, as Nick discovers, a certain justice that "roughly reshapes" or resurrects the very concrete past and links it with the temporal abstraction going by the name of history.

At more than one point in *The Kindly Ones* Nick is caught between these ordering forces of justice and time: justice, not predicated on the moral premises of retribution, but attuned to the classical principles of harmony, broadly social, fundamentally poetic; time, the substance and essence of historical order, allied to the shifting lines of history which are cyclical and finite, parallel and infinite. These two ideas gradually fuse as Nick is transplanted from childhood during the First World War to manhood and maturity in the early weeks of the Second.

The theme of the novel—the regaining of an historic perspective that enables one to revaluate the fluctuating social order and function within it—plays back and forth between these two periods, separated by twenty-five years but linked by their corresponding values. Conscious of this interplay, realizing that the end of one war and the beginning of another have marked crucial stages in his development, Nick would impart a justness to the contingencies and consequences of history, or seek an historic justice in things that have happened. As the last volume in the second trilogy of the series, and capping several decades, *The Kindly Ones* transcends Nick's search for patterns in life and society and becomes most closely woven into the theme of history itself.

Powell gains historic continuity between the first long chapter of the novel (focusing on 1914) and the latter three chapters (covering 1938–39) through the linking motif of the Furies, the mythic goddesses of destruction who terrorized under the name Erinyes ("the angry ones") and were appeased by being addressed as Eumenides ("the kindly ones"). But except in the broadest way, Powell's Furies refuse to translate from myth into religion, philosophy, or even psychology. Rather, they symbolize historic flux, the uneasiness, confusion, madness of the times. The comic turn in *The Kindly Ones*—the overturning of the myth itself—is Powell's sending his Orestes to ferret out the Furies and the problems of society, not the abstractions behind them. If history must repeat itself, the Eumenides really are kindly. One may convert the shadows of the past into the substance of future action.

For the Furies are not to be appeased. At the peak of tense optimism, Europe now begins its descent into holocaust, exploding all hopes of imaginative solutions to problems of power. *The Kindly Ones*, dealing with the beginnings of the two great wars, expands Powell's favorite theme globally, suggesting that power ultimately destroys not only the body, but the body politic. Will and imagination, destruction and propitiation become the antipodes of an historic archetype that resides in the collective methods and conscience of 1938. Chamberlain, the embodiment of the Choephori, moves out to appease the powers that be; Godesberg is transformed into a latter-day Myceneae; and like Agamemnon, Czechoslovakia is betrayed. The lesson that appeasement teaches is simple: it doesn't work.

In the very juxtaposing of these early reactions to the two wars, Powell further implies the responsibility of one era toward another. As he made clear in *Casanova's Chinese Restaurant*, one can learn from ghosts; and in *The Kindly Ones* the specters of the past instruct the present, even though it remains mute, unintelligent, sluggish, or impotent in taking the advice. It is left (as always it seems) for the individual to act, as Nick does. Widmerpool's advent at Stourwater during the *tableaux vivants* of the Seven Deadly Sins (in which Nick is commandeered to play Sloth) and the reactions occasioned by going through Giles's effects at the Bellevue, together quicken at last Nick's awareness of his own responsibility, as the past (Giles's old war citations) calls to the present (Widmerpool's new commission). Each man has his own historic method. For Nick, the casual, rather than violent transitions and revelations spur his quest after Furies who refuse to be packed away in World War I footlockers stored in seedy hotels, lulled into baroque luxury in posh mansions, or kept neurotically pacing the vestibule at Ten Downing Street.

The Kindly Ones closes during a London blackout, on a challenging, yet optimistic, and almost elated note. War must be destructive universally, personally; but it can be reconstructive. The small shocks of life, the reversals, the decisions, the ultimate moves, the conclusions work between two poles. In the novel Nick seeks and finds action; and the Furies, once come, must be engaged, not propitiated. Walking through the darkened streets, he contemplates the realms of action to which he is now committed, "the region beyond the whitecurrant bushes [his boyhood at Stonehurst], where the wild country begins, where armies forever campaign, where the Rules and Discipline of War prevail." [7]

There is little in the subsequent "war trilogy" to harmonize with this appealing, almost poetic note of expectation that closes *The Kindly Ones*. The sense of adventure is soon dissipated in routine and boredom, just as the idea of action itself suffers deflation. "The region beyond," Nick discovers, originates in "the valley of bones," twists over a no-man's-land strewn with memos, minutes, inspections, orders, and counter-orders, and plods up mountains of red tape; campaigning is indeed "forever" but behind company desks, in battalion mess halls, or in general staff corridors; and the "Rules and Discipline of War" prevail through goldbricking, boondoggling, lobbying, simulating, woolgathering, transferring, and (political) maneuvering. Nick's quest through this wasteland of bureaucratic bumph progressively penetrates the façade built around the hollow myth of hero and heroism to disclose what is fallible and best in men caught up in the toils of a nonheroic machine.

In *The Music of Time* the ill-geared, impersonal, desperate, but necessary machine grinds on miles behind the lines, becoming an historic metaphor for the small passions of men who now may dance to drum-taps and bugle calls, but who are fighting another sort of war entirely: the tailor's war; the war of show and bluff; the war of personalities, one-upsmanship, deception; the war of petty vengeances and old scores; the war of manners, protocol, bootlicking, and self-aggrandizement. In short, England at war is not very different from England at peace; war merely concentrates the clash of will and imagination. The imagery of the titles in the trilogy—*The Valley of Bones, The Soldier's Art, The Military Philosophers*—suggests an ascending awareness of the problems of men in conflict with the machine and each other. But with a comedy grown grimmer, and with deepening irony, the novels successively illustrate the disastrous, bathetic responses—political, aesthetic, philosophic—to underlying questions of human values.

The Valley of Bones takes its title from Ezekiel's famous vision—a straight-from-the-shoulder admonition to the Hebrews, dispersed and downtrodden under the Babylonian captivity, to rally themselves and become a nation once again. "And the bones came together, bone to bone. And . . . the sinews and the flesh came upon them, and the skin covered them . . . and the breath came unto them and they lived, and stood up upon their feet, an exceeding great army." Ezekiel's macabre notion of fusion is more legalistic than military, and Powell's use of the title is more literally ironic than symbolic. The disparate entities that come together for the "supreme effort" are disjointed, unrelated—a mass of professions and personalities that must be molded into an effective fighting unit. Like the parched, bleached, scattered bones they must be articulated and fleshed out.

But *The Valley of Bones* is hardly a novel of articulation. The hand and spirit of the Lord are nowhere present. Instead there are men, never strong, often ineffective, seldom secure, always troubled. Ezekiel's allegory depicts the resurrection of a nation; Powell's narrative shows the partial breakdown of an infantry company. Since war is, after all, like any closed society, only the sum total of those who comprise it, so "Rules and Discipline" are only as perfect as those who formulate or execute them—in other words, imperfect, subject to change and chance. These, then, become the modern visions and main themes of the novel: the almost complete collapse of control, accompanied by the gradual revelation that the romantic aura of war is dissipated in its near-classic tediousness.

Powell comes at his themes directly through personality, and the novel is shot through with a humanizing impulse. Something in most men rebels against living by the book, against living an enforced, impossible excellence. Because the majority are basically too human and vulnerable ever to become inhuman and precise, the system, and not really war, becomes their private Waterloo. In the brief, pathetic career of Nick's company commander, Captain Rowland Gwatkin, are concentrated action and symbol. Beginning ostensibly as one of the system's strongest links, Gwatkin ends as one of its weakest, his brittle ideals shattered by experience, his sense of order undermined at last by disenchantment. The world of "officers and gentlemen," he comes to learn, only outwardly glistens with the spit-and-polish of military *noblesse oblige*. Beneath the patina of comradery and Kiplingesque romance are the scarred surfaces of a grubby, routine existence, where success is not easy, where failure is severe, and where one failure seems to lead to a nexus of failures.

Gwatkin's masterminding of incredible snafus is pathetic; it marks him as unfit to command, but also elevates him above those who, fit to command, are dreary, priggish, boring, ludicrous, lifeless, dangerous. His failures are those of imagination (as, later, Widmerpool's outrageous and continuing successes are those of will), for while he may doggedly abide by the superficial sense of order, he cannot forecast changes in the idea of order itself. Order, it becomes apparent, exists because of change, not despite it. Accompanying change is chance, which, in the case of an infantry company within the machine, or a wartime society without, must incorporate personal order into larger patterns of flux. Character still remains fate; yet the often incongruous clashes between them—life's incongruities in general—are never as easily articulated or fleshed out as Ezekiel's bones.

Success throughout *The Music of Time* in articulating this basic incongruity is perhaps greatest in the trilogy dealing with war, and perhaps technically most successful (certainly most successfully conceived) in *The Soldier's Art*. The interplay between private and societal change, between planned direction and chancy diversion, between personal myth and history is viewed through shifting dramatic perspectives that alternately see war as the mere backdrop for the dance, or the actual subject heightening and intensifying the relationships of the dancers. Nor is "dramatic perspectives" a fortuitous

phrase. The principal metaphor of *The Soldier's Art*—
established at the opening when Nick describes his purchase of an army overcoat at a shop dealing in actors'
costumes and officers' supplies—is theatrical. War, with
its various "theatres", its various "stages" of operations,
is truly the "big show." Theatre becomes the grand eu-
phemism for the now-martial dance of life and death, for
war. Both offer the illusion that character spontaneously
controls fate, while in reality it is being moved, driven
by larger forces and by design to an outcome already
foreshadowed—to the shape across the line.

The dramatic metaphor, together with the novel's
central theme—how the soldier practices his art to rise
or fall in the machine—activates the overall aesthetics of
war that go beyond the coarser politics of *The Valley of
Bones*. "Art" may be the science of soldiering, its highest calling; or, of slighter nobility, it is the acquired skill
and dexterity in carrying out certain unpalatable, but
necessary jobs. Again—as Nick frequently discovers—art
reverts to cunning and artifice, the finesse of evasion
rather than engagement. And at its darkest it can represent a contrivance to command—as Widmerpool bears
out in the next volume—powers of life and death.

But the outward changes in people Nick knows, or
changes in meaning of an aesthetic by which they must
now live—changes all the while taking place against the
continuing background of war—are, as always, less disturbing than inward flux. Internalized and idealized, the
soldier's art is to "think first, fight afterwards," rather
than (ironically) to intuitively practice the converse. If
to Childe Roland—the quotation and title come from
the Browning poem—thought means emotional reflection and to Nick it suggests intellectual deliberation,
both are, as far as Powell is concerned, right. The novel
dramatizes "the soldier's art" of thought as imagination
and as will, and is no less concerned with how Nick
adjusts to the thoughts of others; how, like Childe Ro-

land, he must face the ambiguity of an ordeal and the ambiguity of its results.

Concern for the right and wrong way of thinking is not new to *The Music of Time*. What is new, however, is that mere utilitarian considerations of thinking rightly and making a "good" or "safe" choice, thinking wrongly and making a wrong one, or simply not thinking at all have been seriously challenged by moral and ethical considerations. Schoolboy, professional, romantic rivalries—these are no longer the things at stake; life itself is. Thus Widmerpool, still master of the will and ever as strict an exponent of the utilitarian approach to "the soldier's art," forges ahead by hewing close to the lines of discipline and overreaching them when he safely can. Widmerpool's foil—and ultimate scapegoat—is Stringham, now strengthened by his new-found imaginative intelligence. Stringham has become a cynic of the old school, seeking practical virtue through a self-imposed morality that involves freedom from certain responsibilities. But he has not "opted out"; he is sorting out, "trying to get things straight in [his] own mind."

Possessing neither Widmerpool's callous industry nor Stringham's creative cynicism, Nick would seem the least likely to sort things out or get things done. But the total of what Nick appears *not* to do in the novel must be played against the little bit he does well. In the last analysis the novel belongs less to those who seem to have mastered the soldier's art than to Nick who feels himself "without any particular qualifications for practicing [it]." Merely by being thrown together with Widmerpool, Nick rises above him ethically and morally. It is Nick who remains hopeful, concerned, candid, and self-sacrificing in the matter of Private Stringham; and it is Widmerpool who does Stringham in—a bitter lesson to aid in the realization that perhaps the most basic element of the soldier's art is survival.

Powell's aim in *The Soldier's Art* is not, however, to

assert Nick's ethical and moral ascendency over Widmerpool, but to show that he can survive with dignity and honesty intact, on his own terms, yet at the expense of no one else. Nick's character has been continually strengthened by opportunity (as Widmerpool's has been weakened by opportunism), and has enlarged itself until Nick now necessarily dwarfs everyone in *The Music of Time*, even Widmerpool himself. Nick is the one who ultimately realizes that the final and finest expression of the soldier's art means more than remaining human in the face of the dehumanizing processes of war. It means, almost conclusively, remaining human in the face of the more dangerous and impersonal dehumanizing processes of men themselves, who, miles from the front, engage in reduced, but seemingly imperative, social, ethical, and moral struggles.

The Military Philosophers, however, concluding the trilogy and evoking the last years of the war in Europe, pretty thoroughly obliterates the idea that something of value might emerge from these behind-the-lines skirmishes. Any vestiges of the heroic myth originating in *The Valley of Bones* and weakly sustained in *The Soldier's Art* wither under Nick's casual but significant reflections on the end result of any war.

> The dark waters of the Thames below, the beauty of the day, brought to mind the lines about Stetson and the ships at Mylae, how death had undone so many. . . . Barnby was no longer available to repaint his frescoes. Death had undone him. It looked as if death might have undone Stringham too.[8]

The war has, in fact, undone at least a dozen of the old guard, and left more bones bleaching in the valley. Not coincidentally is Ezekiel the prophet of Powell's war trilogy as well as Eliot's poem. Eliot's symbolic wasteland, however, which once stood a fair (if not overly great) chance of revival, has become a literal wasteland denuded of its key figures. War, obviously, is one way of killing off characters; but Powell is hardly being arbitrary. War does kill; war does ravage, irreparably, at times finally.

But here, as elsewhere, Powell champions life over death. As the offstage tragedies grow greater—indeed, as history stoutly marches toward crises and holocaust—the onstage comedy swells. The grimmest, at times most elegiac of all his novels, *The Military Philosophers* may well be one of his wittiest. It caps a trilogy which, in retrospect, might be taken as a comic-epic *Iliad*—framed in red tape, complete with mock battles, histrionics, gods from the machine, inversions, and parodies of mythical allusions—were it made clear, too, how it is sensitively attuned to the desperate temper of the times and to the now-feverish dance of death.

The tragicomedy emerges from the head-on clash between the realpolitik of war and any absurd notions of residual philosophizing that might sway military passions. Prophets, at least of the military sort, are only a rank away from the "military philosophers," and the route from one to the other easily managed if one accepts detours through ironies and oxymorons. Inspiration has been replaced by mechanical response, the bright ladder of intelligence by the chain of command; wisdom has become guesswork; logic has turned into logistics, and truth into expediency. War offers only one viable philosophy—after survival—summarized in the memorable laconicism of Powell's Field Marshal (a very thinly disguised Montgomery) when he cautions the Belgian attaché against allowing the Brussels Resistance band to snafu Allied movements through the Low Countries: "If they . . . give trouble . . . I'll shoot 'em up. Is that clear? Shoot 'em up!" Such (more or less) is the noble philosophy by which Widmerpool gets rid of

Stringham and Templer, inheriting Stringham's money by marrying his niece, who also happens to have been Templer's ex-mistress. To the last resounding thwack, war has confirmed the man of will's "shoot 'em up" philosophy, and proved Widmerpool not only unfunny and odious, but dangerous and destructive. No amount of comedy can redeem the tragedy of a world that has Widmerpools to run it.

Powell, however, is not writing fiction of redemption, but trying to remain doubly faithful to the justness of history and to his comic view of it. If the dance has sustained itself until now, and many of the dancers have danced so far, it is because the actions of becoming—and whether one becomes a Widmerpool or Jenkins is quite beside the point—are more concrete spokesmen for such justness than any abstract theorizing possibly could be. And if Powell still continues to be fascinated by double-dealing, dishonor, bureaucratic idiocy, and inhumanity, it is because the comic writer must persist in his belief that the "past, just as the present, had to be accepted for what it thought and what it was." These are Nick's words toward the end of *The Military Philosophers*, perhaps the key to the highest philosophy of the sequence as a whole, but certainly at one with his symbolic acceptance of GI underwear at the novel's very end. Together, thought and gesture suggest partial acknowledgment of the continuity among period, epoch, and phase, with the further recognition that some things must be sloughed off, given up, even lost.

In *The Music of Time* each phase of the dance, taken step by step, is rendered complete and in its entirety. Yet as Nick moves horizontally a notch on the temporal ladder, and a notch vertically on the spatial one, the rounding off of any single phase is but a continuation of the phases gone before. One movement of the dance ends; another begins; but the dance itself has never really been interrupted at all. Over these nine volumes—and undoubtedly in the trilogy to come—Powell has not only shown awareness of the ways in which the individual changes against the sameness of time, but how (in Nick's words) "the sequence of inevitable sameness that follows a person through life" plays against time's flux. Powell's genius, it seems, lies in the ability to invert these basic conditions without sacrificing meaning or character; to compel the realization, by means of his historic vision and his comic control, that both the random movements of life and the patterned movements of the dance can be seen as the perfect movement of art. A *Dance to the Music of Time* may well be the twentieth-century paradigm of the novel sequence that harmonizes most fully with the shifting and complex nature of continuance and change.

Notes

1 – Doris Lessing

Novels in the *Children of Violence* sequence are: *Martha Quest* (1952), *A Proper Marriage* (1954), *A Ripple from the Storm* (1958), *Landlocked* (1965), *The Four-Gated City* (1969).

1. "The Small Personal Voice," in *Declaration*, ed. T. Maschler (London: MacGibbon and Kee, 1957), p. 47.
2. *Martha Quest* (New York: The New American Library, Signet Books, 1966), p. 17.
3. *The Four-Gated City* (New York: Alfred A. Knopf, 1969), pp. 485–86.
4. Hannah Arendt, "Reflections on Violence," *New York Review of Books*, February 27, 1969, pp. 19–20.
5. Ibid., p. 30.
6. *Landlocked* (New York: Simon and Schuster, 1966), p. 462.
7. Arthur Miller, "Battle of Chicago: from the Delegates Side," *New York Times Magazine*, September 15, 1968, p. 29.
8. *Four-Gated City*, p. 198.
9. Ibid., p. 430.
10. Ibid., p. 489.
11. *The Golden Notebook* (New York: McGraw-Hill, 1963), p. 404.
12. Father Alfred Augustine Carey, O. F. M., "Doris Lessing: The Search for Reality, a Study of the Major Themes in Her Novels," Diss. University of Wisconsin, 1964, p. 102.

13. *Four-Gated City*, pp. 369–70.
14. *Landlocked*, p. 386.
15. *Four-Gated City*, p. 133.
16. Ibid., p. 559.

2 – Olivia Manning

Novels in the *Balkan Trilogy* are: *The Great Fortune* (1960), *The Spoilt City* (1962), *Friends and Heroes* (1965).

1. *The Great Fortune* (London: Heinemann, 1960), p. 180.
2. Ibid., p. 79.
3. Ibid., p. 162.
4. Ibid., p. 280.
5. *The Spoilt City* (London: Heinemann, 1962), p. 193.
6. Ibid., p. 240.
7. Ibid., p. 233.
8. Ibid., pp. 109–10.
9. *Friends and Heroes* (London: Heinemann, 1965), p. 179.
10. Ibid., p. 70.

3 – Lawrence Durrell

Novels in the *Alexandria Quartet* are: *Justine* (1957), *Balthazar* (1958), *Mountolive* (1959), *Clea* (1960).

1. *Balthazar* (New York: Dutton, 1958), pp. 14–15.
2. *Clea* (New York: Dutton, 1960), pp. 135–36.
3. Ibid., p. 103.
4. *Justine* (New York: Dutton, 1957), p. 175.
5. *Clea*, p. 177.
6. For locus of these and subsequent quotations from Arnauti's *Moeurs* see *Justine*, pp. 75 ff.
7. For locus of these and subsequent quotations of Pursewarden on art, imagination, and history see *Clea*, pp. 125 ff.
8. *Balthazar*, p. 226.
9. *Mountolive* (New York: Dutton, 1959), p. 215.
10. *Clea*, p. 23.

4–Anthony Burgess

Novels in the *Malayan Trilogy* (*The Long Day Wanes*) are: *Time for a Tiger* (1956), *The Enemy in the Blanket* (1958), *Beds in the East* (1959).

1. Preface to *Nostromo* by Joseph Conrad (New York: Random House, The Modern Library, 1951), p. xxxiii.
2. *Beds in the East* (London: Pan Books, 1964), p. 242.
3. Ibid., p. 333.
4. Ibid., p. 509.
5. *The Enemy in the Blanket* (London: Pan Books, 1964), p. 295.
6. *Time for a Tiger* (London: Pan Books, 1964), p. 160.
7. *Enemy in the Blanket*, p. 222.
8. *Beds in the East*, pp. 451–52.
9. Ibid., p. 474.
10. *Enemy in the Blanket*, p. 175.
11. *Time for a Tiger*, p. 42.
12. Ibid., p. 49.
13. *Beds in the East*, p. 347.
14. *Time for a Tiger*, p. 38.

5–C. P. Snow

Novels in the *Strangers and Brothers* sequence are: *Strangers and Brothers* (1940), *The Light and the Dark* (1947), *Time of Hope* (1949), *The Masters* (1951), *The New Men* (1954), *Homecoming* (1956), *The Conscience of the Rich* (1958), *The Affair* (1960), *Corridors of Power* (1964), *The Sleep of Reason* (1968), *Last Things* (1970).

1. "The Two Cultures," *New Statesman and Nation*, 52 (October 6, 1956), 413–14.
2. "Science, Politics, and the Novelist," *Kenyon Review*, 23 (Winter, 1961), 6.
3. "Challenge to the Intellect," *Times Literary Supplement*, August 15, 1958, p. iii.
4. Author's Note to *The Conscience of the Rich* (London: Macmillan, 1958), p. vii–viii.

5. *Time of Hope* (New York: Scribner's, 1949), p. 46.

6. "Books and Writers," *Spectator*, 186 (January 19, 1951), 82.

7. *The Light and the Dark* (New York: Scribner's, 1947), p. 383.

8. *Strangers and Brothers* (New York: Scribner's, 1960), p. 53.

9. *Homecoming* (New York: Scribner's, 1956), p. 226.

10. "Science, Politics, and the Novelist," p. 11.

11. *Homecoming*, p. 136.

12. *The Masters* (New York: Scribner's, 1951), p. 196.

13. Ibid., p. 161.

14. *The Sleep of Reason* (New York: Scribner's, 1968), p. 445.

6 – Anthony Powell

Novels in the as yet uncompleted *A Dance to the Music of Time* sequence are: *A Question of Upbringing* (1951), *A Buyer's Market* (1953), *The Acceptance World* (1955), *At Lady Molly's* (1957), *Casanova's Chinese Restaurant* (1960), *The Kindly Ones* (1962), *The Valley of Bones* (1964), *The Soldier's Art* (1966), *The Military Philosophers* (1968).

1. *A Buyer's Market* (Boston: Little, Brown, 1955), p. 254.

2. *The Acceptance World* (Boston: Little, Brown, 1955), pp. 212–13.

3. *A Question of Upbringing* (Boston: Little, Brown, 1955), p. 2.

4. *The Kindly Ones* (London: Heinemann, 1962), p. 180.

5. The first chapter of *The Kindly Ones* breaks the chronology of the sequence. See below, p. 143.

6. *Casanova's Chinese Restaurant* (London: Heinemann, 1960), p. 229.

7. *The Kindly Ones*, p. 254.

8. *The Military Philosophers* (Boston: Little, Brown, 1968), p. 113.

Index

Arendt, Hannah, xvi, 14, 15
Austen, Jane, 53

Bergson, Henri, 85, 133
Bildungsroman, 1, 10, 85
Broch, Herman, 2
Browning, Robert, 150
Burgess, Anthony: his hero's view of history, xv; disillusion and disintegration in sequence, xvi; heterogeneity of Malaya, 30; his hero caught in history, 73, 74; themes in trilogy, 73; views on imperialism compared to Waugh's and Orwell's, 73; use of setting compared to that in other sequences, 74; sources of cyclical theory of history, 75; on change and history, 79; characters, 84; style, 85; his sequence as drama of change, 89
—*Beds in the East*, 76, 77; *Clockwork Orange, A*, 18, 120; *Enemy in the Blanket, The*, 77; *Malayan Trilogy, The* (*The Long Day Wanes*), xv, xix, 71–91; *Time for a Tiger*, 77, 82

Camus, Albert, 105

Carey, Father John, 19
Conrad, Joseph, 71, 72

Durrell, Lawrence: art linked to history, xix; concern with revolution, xix; motif and imagery in sequence, xix; treatment of artist compared with Powell's, xix; heterogeneity of locale, 30; respect for history, 48; themes in sequence, 51; narrative devices in sequence, 53; sequence as attempt at "pure novel," 54; art and the artist, 56; use of mirror imagery in sequence, 57–60 passim; use of theory of relativity in sequence, 58; history distinguished from art, 60; use of history in *Mountolive*, 66; genesis of artist, 69
—*Alexandria Quartet, The*, xix, 51–69, 74, 81, 107, 109, 112; *Balthazar*, 52; *Clea*, 63; *Justine*, 55, 59, 67, 69; *Mountolive*, 66–68 passim

Einstein, Albert, 85, 133, 134
Eliot, George, 53

161